T0193216

VOICES *of the* SOUL

THE SONG OF TRANSFORMATION

DR. BARBARA BYERS

WESTBOW
PRESS®
A DIVISION OF THOMAS NELSON
& ZONDERVAN

WestBow Press books may be ordered through booksellers or by contacting:

WestBow Press
A Division of Thomas Nelson & Zondervan
1663 Liberty Drive
Bloomington, IN 47403
www.westbowpress.com
844-714-3454

ISBN: 978-1-6642-9706-7 (sc)
ISBN: 978-1-6642-9707-4 (hc)
ISBN: 978-1-6642-9705-0 (e)

Library of Congress Control Number: 2023906480

Print information available on the last page.

WestBow Press rev. date: 05/25/2023

SAGE PUBLISHING: Excerpts from *Jonathan Edwards on Beauty, Desire and the Sensory World* by Belden C. Lane, copyright 2004. Reprinted with permission from Sage Publishing.

SCEPTER PUBLISHERS: Excerpts from *In the School of the Holy Spirit* by Jacques Philippe, copyright 2007. Reprinted with permission from Scepter Publishers.

SCEPTER PUBLISHERS: Excerpts from *The Way of Trust and Love* by Jacques Philippe, copyright 2011. Reprinted with permission from Scepter Publishers. [For more information about Fr. Jacques Philippe's books, as well as speaking events, visit https://www.frjacquesphilippe.com.]

SIMON & SCHUSTER: Excerpts from *Jesus Feminist: An Invitation to Revisit the Bible's View of Women* by Sarah Bessey, copyright 2013. Reprinted with permission from Simon & Schuster, Inc.

ST PAULS: Excerpts from *Searching for and Maintaining Peace* by Jacques Philippe, 2002. Reprinted with permission ST PAULS.

What people are saying about *Voices of the Soul*

Dr. Byers is an incredible gift to the body of Christ. Throughout her ministry career, and especially in this book, she brings the perfect balance of psychological understanding and biblical truth. If you want to better understand the anatomy of your soul and how it is formed, malformed, and transformed, buy this book and dive into its brilliance. Dr. Byers is my friend and a trusted voice in my life. I invite you to allow her to become a trusted voice in your life, too.

Dr. Jon Chasteen
President, The King's University
Lead Pastor, Victory Church
Author, *Half the Battle: Healing Your Hidden Hurts*

God wants to give you something amazing that money can't buy: wholeness and holiness in your soul! *Voices of the Soul* shows you how to let God be the architect of your soul and how to partner with him in building a beautiful masterpiece. This book will help uncover the stuck parts of your inner self—including anxiety, anger, grief, and unforgiveness—so God can free up those areas for full partnership with him. Let Dr. Barbara Byers serve as your guide on this journey of transformation, and experience the joy, peace and wholeness God has designed for you as his image-bearer.

Jimmy Evans
Founder and President, XO Marriage
Author, *Marriage on the Rock*

In ***Voices of the Soul***, Dr. Byers has written a scholarly, yet practical, study of the soul that is useful for Bible study groups, classroom presentations and personal Bible study. The Bibliography reveals the depth of research behind this writing. Without reservation, I recommend *Voices of the Soul* to all theological students, to pastors and teachers, and especially to Christian believers committed to a deeper understanding of their faith in Christ.

Tommy H. Briggs, Sr.
Gateway Church Network Care Pastor

Dr. Byers understands and explains the capacity of the soul like no other. I especially treasure her explanations concerning the "will"—trust me, these are gold. This anointed book is not about knowledge alone; it is packed with wisdom and practical insight that can be life-changing when applied to your soul and your life.

Rebecca Wilson LCSW, LMFT
Associate pastor (ret.), Gateway Church

CONTENTS

Dedication xv
Preface.. xvii

1 – Introduction... 1

Part I: Voices of Knowing and Choosing

2 – The Will.. 17
3 – The Rational Mind 30
4 – The Receptive Mind.. 47
5 – The Conscience.. 61

Part II: Voices of Energy and Motivation

6 – Emotions... 77
7 – Desire... 92
8 – Appetites 107

Part III: Voices of Being and Formation

9 – Sense of Being... 125
10 – Masculine and Feminine 140
11 – Character 155
12 – Concluding Thoughts 169

Acknowledgements.. 179
Bibliography... 181

DEDICATION

To my children and grandchildren.
May you know God's transforming presence.

PREFACE

Considering the Soul

Charles H. Spurgeon said this about the soul: God is "the owner of my inmost passions, the possessor and owner of my secret self."[1] This book invites you to consider the different aspects of the "secret self," the soul, and how the soul is transformed and set aflame for the Lord's glory. As we explore the capacities of the soul, each of the voices of these different aspects of the soul will be explained—both how they are formed and how they are authentically transformed. The way these dimensions are interconnected will give us understanding as we partner with the Lord in our own healing and formation.

Spiritual formation is the Spirit-led process of being changed and conformed to Christlikeness in the deepest places of our souls. As each dimension of the soul is transformed in Christlikeness, true spiritual formation happens. We really are changed!

There are no formulas for spiritual formation because it unfolds in response to the Lord's initiative. We place ourselves under his care and invite his healing into every facet of our souls. Rather than devise our own plans for self-improvement and self-cultivation, we cooperate with him as he reveals our darkness, wounds, and misbeliefs and invites us into the light of his truth. It's our inner lives he's after because all the issues of our lives flow from there. As we recognize the importance of his initiative and our responses, we can ask him to increase our spiritual alertness so we can choose to walk victoriously. We need to learn to lean in and pick up

---

[1] Charles H. Spurgeon, "Psalm 139" in *The Treasury of David*, accessed February 15, 2022, https://archive.spurgeon.org/treasury/ps139.php.

his heartbeat. The more we recognize him and know his heart, the more we can respond and become like him. It is in beholding him that we are changed.

Where We Are Going

James Clerk Maxwell was a brilliant Scottish physicist who loved the Lord, scripture, and mathematics. He spoke about "undreamt of regions," the underlying realities in the realm of physics.[2] I love that phrase and hope in this book to explore the "undreamt of regions" of the soul, so vast and beautiful, but often so hidden and unknown. As we explore these regions, we will understand the capacities of our souls, each with a voice, and be able to collaborate with the Lord in our spiritual formation.

We all have broken places where we need the Lord's healing and deep transformation. This book will explain the interactive, nonlinear nature of that process, and also:

- help you understand how the soul is created and composed, and how it functions;
- aid you in setting in order what is wounded and disordered, and what may be blocking your growth; and
- help you mature where you are immature, bringing about transformation as you become a "masterpiece of harmony" by the power of the Holy Spirit.

Although the soul is not linear in its dimensions, for clarity each facet of the soul is separated out and then interrelated as part of the whole soul, delineating how we can move forward in intentional ways to build the soul. In Part I, the instruments of knowing and choosing are introduced: the will, the rational mind, the receptive mind, and the conscience. In Part II, the energies and motivations that propel us—emotions, desires, and appetites—are outlined. In Part III, the formation of the soul is

---

[2] James Clerk Maxwell, quoted in a sermon by Kris Vallotton, August 2, 2021, at Bethel Church, Redding, CA.

discussed, including these engagements: a sense of being, the masculine and feminine, and character.

As you read this book, I encourage you to linger in each chapter to answer the "Pause and Reflect" questions so that you can consider what the Lord is doing in each aspect of your soul. Prayerful attention to the questions will propel you along in the transformation process.

What Do You Desire?

At the onset of this study on the soul's spiritual formation, will you choose to let God meet you in these chapters any way he desires? We can't attain our own righteousness, but we can surrender and invite him to burn out the old ways and fill us with himself. As we step into our first chapter, before you know anything about what he might say or do through these words, will you give him permission? Will you agree with heaven? The Lord is the lover of our souls. He comes to make us whole, to call us out of our slumber, to give our souls their being and well-being. The thing to do when he speaks is to say a whole-hearted yes.

Prayer

Thank you, Lord, as I begin this study, that I have the Holy Spirit as my guide and counselor. I ask you to set a fire in me during this time to burn away the old and burn in the new. Enlighten and heal me. Make my feet sturdy to walk in your paths. Draw me to you that I may run with you and know your love as never before in my soul.

Set in me a holy expectancy that you will meet me as I seek to understand my "secret self." Lord Jesus, change my life and make me whole. With Psalm 103:1, I say, "Praise the Lord, my soul, all my inmost being, praise his holy name (NIV)." Thank you, Lord, that you forgive my sins, heal my diseases, and redeem my life, crowning me with your love. Bless the Lord, oh my soul!

With the writer of Psalm 139 I invite your searching gaze into my heart and I welcome your deep healing.

> *… Examine me through and through;*
> *find out everything that may be hidden within me.*
> *Put me to the test and sift through all my anxious cares.*
> *See if there is any path of pain I'm walking on,*
> *and lead me back to your glorious, everlasting way—*
> *the path that brings me back to you.*
> *—Ps 139: 23–24 TPT*

Pause and Reflect

Take a few minutes now and write out what you desire from the Lord as you enter this study. What do you want him to do? What have you been considering in your heart that you would like the Lord to heal? Are you aware even now of areas that need change? He longs to encounter you there.

> *Pause at the threshold*
> *Of the sacred space;*
> *Bow low.*
> *Prepare for fresh*
> *Encounter*
> *With the Holy One.*

> *"Entrance," in Watching for the Kingfisher by Ann Lewin*

1

INTRODUCTION

Jesus is the lover of our souls and fully understands them. All power is his to heal and change them. "Long before he laid down earth's foundations, he had us in mind, had settled on us as the focus of his love, to be made whole and holy by his love" (Eph 1:4 MSG). The love of God is so high, so deep, so wide, so broad, so limitless, so searching, so drawing … a love coming to meet us. It doesn't dry up or fade away or fail. It is never indifferent. The Lord waits for us to acknowledge and receive this love. The apostle John wrote, "See what an incredible quality of love the Father has shown to us, that we would [be permitted to] be named *and* called *and* counted the children of God! And so we are!" (1 Jn 3:1 AMP).

God's love is the greatest reality we will ever experience. It is strong, mighty, faithful, full of promise, restorative, undiminished in the face of our sins, passionate, pursuing, untamed, penetrating, and captivating. We are no longer outcasts or orphans, for we have been ransomed by holy love. Fr. Romano Guardini wrote, "He is the Living One, the Close One, the One forever drawing near in holy freedom. He is the lover who not only operates, but specifically acts in love."[3]

We can be confident that the Lord knows all about us and really sees us yet still accepts us as we are. Psalm 139 assures us of this: "Lord, you know everything there is to know about me. You perceive every movement of my heart and soul, and you understand my every thought before it even enters my mind. You are so intimately aware of me, Lord. You read my heart like

---

[3] Romano Guardini, *The Lord* (originally published 1954; repr., Washington, DC: Gateway Editions, 1982), 125.

an open book. … You've gone into my future to prepare the way, and in kindness you follow behind me to spare me from the harm of my past. … Wherever I go, your hand will guide me; your strength will empower me" (Ps 139:1–5, 10 TPT).

Theologians call this "prevenient love." *Pre* means "before": God's love comes before our need for his forgiveness, his help, his wisdom, his redemption. He has it all waiting ahead of us. The word *prevenient* also means "producing a sense of anticipation." We long with anticipation to experience his goodness. He wants us to know his goodness, and he promises he will meet us: "My God in his steadfast love will meet me" (Ps 59:10 NRSV). And his promise can never fail.

Pause and Reflect

Do you really know, believe, and receive God's love? Do you know that he is love? Ask him to reveal himself to you in that way. Ask him now: Lord, reveal yourself; reveal your deep love. As your Word says, may I come to know and believe the love you have for me (see 1 Jn 4:16).

Our Souls

Since Christ loves us and died for us, he wants us to value our souls. But we often don't understand the capacities of our souls, and so we fail to understand how we are to grow, heal, and truly live. This book should help in that understanding, bringing clarity so our true, genuine, and redeemed voices can be expressed.

Scripture refers to the soul in many places. Sometimes interchangeable words are used (such as *heart, mind, inner man,* and *spirit*) to refer to our inner depths. According to *Young's Analytical Concordance,* the Hebrew word *nephesh,* usually translated as "soul," is used hundreds of times in the Old Testament. The ancient Jewish people saw the central idea of the soul as the whole person. For instance, Deuteronomy 26:16 instructs them to observe the Lord's decrees "with all your heart and with all your soul" (NIV). "Heart" and "soul" are not meant to be understood as two separate organs but as inseparable and interchangeable. In the New Testament, the word *psychē* is usually translated as "soul." We find this in 1 Thessalonians 5:23: "I pray God your whole spirit and soul and body be preserved blameless unto the coming of our Lord Jesus Christ" (KJV).

It's not that we *have* souls like something we carry along with us, but that we *are* souls. Willard wrote:

> The soul is that aspect of your whole being that *correlates,*
> *integrates,* and *enlivens* everything going on in the various
> dimensions of the self. It is the life center of the human
> being. … which gives strength, direction, and harmony to
> every other element of our life. … When we are speaking
> of the soul, then, we are speaking of the *deepest level of life*
> *and power* in the human being.[4]

Soul is a concise word that expresses the union of all the inner powers within a person's being. Payne wrote of the soul as "the center … from which emotions, thought, motivations, courage and action spring—the wellspring of life."[5] It's our whole personality and personhood, what makes us distinct, definite persons. Our souls are gifts given to us by God to be ourselves. We should deeply esteem and care for these gifts.

King David declared, "Bless the Lord, O my soul, and all that is within me, bless his holy name" (Ps 103:1 NRSV). The soul is simply shorthand for "all that is within me." It is my whole being, all my inner powers, all my capacities and faculties (such as the rational mind, will, imagination, emotions, and conscience), overlapping and working together. Though these parts aren't fully separate and distinct, it is helpful to look at them distinctly, as an anatomy of the soul and its systems.

Transformation Process

We can't grow in the Lord unless we partner with him and allow him to deal with what's in our souls. Jesus is the one who searches our minds and hearts and knows all that is within us (see Rv 2:23). As we grow and

---

[4] Dallas Willard, *Renovation of the Heart* (Colorado Springs, CO: NavPress, 2002), 199.
[5] Leanne Payne, *The Healing Presence* (originally published 1989, repr., Grand Rapids, MI: Hamewith Books, an Imprint of Baker Book House Company, 1995), 161.

experience real transformation, we become mature and complete. Our God becomes the center of our being, literally indwelling us. He is the living vine from which we take in life. He radiates up through our entire being, granting us holy emotions, holy intuition, holy imagination, holy intellect—transforming everything within. The more we understand and practice this truth, the more we mature. His presence makes our souls' formation and transformation possible.

Invitation to the Indwelling God

How do we trust the Holy Spirit to transform us in our weaknesses and limitations, and all the disappointments with self that we carry? We welcome him into every part of our souls, inviting him to come and re-form what has been malformed, create what is lacking in us, and bring to fullness what is dwarfed. This is the crux of these teachings: Christ dwells within, in the central place of our being, and initiates our transformation. He radiates through and into every part of our soul, filling and healing us. Our spiritual lives are formed in the atmosphere of resurrection wonder as we collaborate with his working.

In all our imperfections, the Lord is present. He is greater than us and he is building something wonderful that looks like himself. He likes being with us in the struggle of this. He really does! His grace keeps drawing us. We must stay in the process and persevere. We have to begin to believe and practice his empowering presence. This is not about self-improvement, running our own show, or striving after righteousness. It's about the Lord entering in and transforming us. When we strive, we want him to help us, but he wants to come in and do much, much more.

Wonderfully, he has already transformed the deepest place: we have been saved because he paid the price with his sacrifice on the cross. He was delivered up for us, and now he lives within. Inside, deep in our spirits, we were born anew. This is his gift, and we can receive it with awe and gratitude. Our salvation is the beginning.

We take our place with Jesus in his death. Our old selves go to the grave and we arise new, ready to be his disciples, filled with his life. But there's the rub. How do we make that a continuing reality so that his life and light are evident in us? While we now have the capacity to live abundantly, filled with his life, we are newborns at first, with the facility to grow and eventually to mature. This capacity, this wonderful possibility, is present; the development is not. In God's order of creation, development and formation are necessary.

God wants to enlarge our capacity to know him so we can develop, thrive, and mature. To do this, he has to reveal what hinders us—our propensities to jealousy, self-promotion, anger, pride, impatience, self-deception, self-protection, and all the old patterns of responses. He wants to change our very way of being! This means we don't try to fix ourselves. Instead, we die to our old ways and come alive to God's, exchanging our ways for his. We collaborate with his Spirit in this deep work. He does it all in mercy. His ways don't dishearten us but unfold our real condition.

From Fragmentation to Wholeness

A soul, "like a city that is broken into and without walls" (Prv 25:28 NASB), may be fragmented from painful experiences. The pain of unhealed memories may contain messages of rejection, unworthiness, lack, hopelessness, and depression, all of which silence or mute our true voices. But the Lord is able to heal the deepest pains that paralyze our emotional well-being and stifle and stymie our spiritual formation. The Lord enters our sin-marred memories with his light and healing presence so we can be restored.

Our hearts have created messages around past wounding experiences and our choices in response to those experiences. These experiences form us and our interpretations of life, many times apart from our awareness and understanding. The deep places in our souls are complex and subtle and each has had a life of its own, developing apart from God. But God can penetrate the deepest layers, every part. He knows our depths, and he knows how to reshape what has been misshapen and malformed. We receive and enter that work by faith, trusting his grace.

Our natural human life is invaded by a supernatural life. This changes everything. There is already a whole center within us, where Christ dwells, and it is from that complete and whole place that his life will enter into every part of our souls. We come from an already complete, whole place. We are his habitation. Christ is in us, forming himself in us, creating the real persons we are.

Christ sees us complete in him (Col 2:10). As Willard wrote, "Our life in him is whole and blessed, no matter what has or has not been done to us, no matter how shamefully our human circles of sufficiency have been violated."[6] This should give us such hope. St. Augustine, drawing from Song of Solomon 2:9–10, framed it this way: "He looked through the lattice of our flesh and he spake us fair."[7] God has already implanted real good within us! We are his fair ones, complete, and yet still in formation. We don't have to strive for this. We simply receive, and then we collaborate in his formation.

Journey to Connection

After our salvation, transformation isn't easy or automatic. When Paul was arrested by the Spirit on the Damascus Road, it was the beginning of his new life in Christ, but his spiritual formation took many years of coming aside with the Lord, being tested and baptized with truth again and again before he was mature enough to be anointed for ministry. More development was necessary.

We don't always see what has influence over our thoughts and motives, what lies below the surface of consciousness. But God knows what is unseen, unnoticed, unfinished. Only God knows all the hidden dimensions within us. Only God has the power to change us from the inside. The more we understand where we are disconnected, the more we can cooperate with the Holy Spirit's activity within. As we ask, God brings to light the brokenness within our souls. Like a good doctor, he initiates a cleansing process that can begin to get the infection out. It may be painful for a season, for "painful dying to the old life precedes entry

---

[6] Willard, *Renovation of the Heart*, 194.

[7] St. Augustine, *Confessions*, Volume II: Books 9–13 trans. William Watts, Loeb Classical Library 27 (Cambridge, MA: Harvard University Press, 1912), 406–7.

into the new."[8] We may become anxious as we live against the old dictates of our defense system.

As we begin to see what is amiss and ask him to bring healing, we must be willing to face some matters in the process of healing. "We cannot begin inner transformation unless we're open to change. Yet most of us are resistant to any form of alteration."[9] Often that is because of the pain and risks involved. As we become willing to face the pain, four important themes emerge:

- **Anxiety.** We have to face anxiety and let it come up so that we can process the pain that has been driving it, including trauma. We will need to stop covering our anxiety with busyness and numbing. That deeper pain that has been feeding anxiety and depression can be healed when we allow ourselves to feel and name it.

- **Anger.** We have to face anger over perceived injustices. In particular, we have to face repressed anger that we may not want to admit—even anger toward God, or toward ourselves, which we often transfer onto others.

- **Grief.** We have to face grief and the misery of our losses and heartaches. Grieving is really a process of letting go of losses. It is God's process to guide us into health. Appropriate grief is a pain that heals, cleansing the old, preparing us to receive new things.

- **Forgiveness.** We have to forgive by canceling debts against us, relinquishing vengeance, choosing good toward others, and extending mercy. It opens us to God's healing and binds the offender's sins away from us. The moment we will to forgive, God's strength begins to pour into us. We can then stand free from the pain of others by forgiving them and releasing our judgments against them.[10]

---

[8] Frank Lake, *Clinical Theology, Abridged* by Martin H. Yeomans (New York: Crossroad, 1987), 27.

[9] Barbara Shlemon Ryan, *Healing the Hidden Self* (originally published 1982; repr., Notre Dame, IN: Ave Maria Press, 2005), 125.

[10] Mark Pertuit, lecture at the School of Pastoral Care Ministries, Wheaton, IL, July 27, 2010.

Forgiving others and ourselves is foundational to our growth; not to forgive is a barrier. Pain is not optional, but bitterness is. God knows that forgiveness will release and bless us. If we choose to forgive, we prevent our offender from shaping us as victim. Rather we look toward God's favor in our future. We also take responsibility for our own emotions and reactions and decide we will not become the victim, defined by our wounds. We can rewrite our history by collaborating with the Lord's grace, choosing to forgive and to bless the one who wounded us.

Constructing a Soul

We are souls, and by coming into relationship with the Lord, our souls are inhabited by his Holy Spirit, who brings new life. He gives us the capacity to be like him in a real way, to build our lives in him. Oswald Chambers wrote, "Many of us prefer to stay at the threshold of the Christian life instead of going on to construct a soul in accordance with the new life God has put within. We fail because we are ignorant of the way we are made."[11]

We may be ignorant of how our souls function, and thus how to respond in cooperation with the Lord. But why did Chambers use the language "construct a soul?" Because we have to *form* a soul around Christ and in partnership with him. We have to *develop* a soul while often deconstructing the faulty one that's been built. We carefully cultivate our souls as he is remaking us. He wonderfully empowers us in this, but we need to take responsibility for constructing a soul, and we need to know we can do it.

Colossians 2:6–7 exhorts, "… You received Christ Jesus, the Master; now *live* him. You're deeply rooted in him. You're well-constructed upon him" (MSG). God has already implanted real good within us! Our part is to receive this. We don't strive for it, but we have collaborative work to do. Proverbs 24:30–31 says: "I went past the field of a sluggard, past the vineyard of someone who has no sense; thorns had come up everywhere, the ground was covered with weeds, and the stone wall was in ruins" (NIV). What a picture of a ruined soul! Often, we have these ruined places

---

[11] Oswald Chambers, *My Utmost for His Highest* (New York: Dodd, Mead & Company, 1935), 141.

because, "The enemy has damaged everything within the sanctuary" (Ps 74:3 AMP). Now we must arise and tend our hearts and allow him to rebuild our sanctuary.

We have responsibility and authority to take "possession" of our souls here and now. But we often don't take that possession because we don't understand the connections between how we act and how we think, between the unconscious parts of us and the conscious parts, between the various interdependent faculties of our souls. The Lord wants us to understand and pursue him in these things. He is constantly working to re-form and construct us according to his idea of how he's made us. He sees every ruined place, everything that is missing within, and can identify them for us. We need to know how to cooperate with this.

The key to transformation is the fullness of knowing him as he is and receiving his love. We need to start thinking differently and live in the fullness of the goodness of God. In the cross and resurrection, we have been given everything we need for transformation. The wonderful news is that everything wrong about us died on the cross with Christ and our righteousness is imparted by his resurrection life. It's the mystery of his deep indwelling that enables us to look like him, that calls us to spiritual formation.

According to Willard, "Spiritual formation ... refers to the Spirit-driven process of forming the inner world of the self in such a way that it becomes like the inner being of Christ."[12] This process is interactive: the Spirit within us, forming our souls with our collaboration. It is his initiative, but it is a very active process for us. For example, we can earnestly pray that he will change and rearrange things within so that we are enabled by his grace to obey him. We seek him, and he answers us. When he answers, we move forward in obedience to what he is showing us or asking of us. Each decision like this propels new growth.

Jesus said, "The person who has my commandments and obeys them is the one who loves me. The one who loves me will be loved by my Father, and I will love him and will reveal myself to him" (Jn 14:21 NET). To those who obey him, an intimacy develops with him where we know and are known, love and are loved. Jesus discloses himself to us. J. I. Packer

---

[12] Willard, *Renovation of the Heart*, 22.

wrote, "All my knowledge of Him depends on His sustained initiative in knowing me. I know Him, because He first knew me, and continues to know me."[13] The Lord initiates, and we respond in loving obedience.

Pause and Reflect

Have you ever considered the idea of constructing a soul? What does this mean to you? What new things would you like to construct in your soul?

Masterpieces

When we are connected to the Spirit, we have power beyond anything we can dream or imagine. Our true selves have incredible capacity for growth and creativity. But we also have an impostor within who covers up the truth, hides, and presents a false front. A good foundation can't be built on what is false, but only on the very life of Christ. That's why Jesus said that we have to lose our lives to find them (see Mt 10:38–39). We must die to our souls' old ways of seeing and doing life, rooted in our inner systems. We are hindered developmentally until his grace comes to set us free. Things in our past may have caused us to turn a certain way and stop our good development, but we don't have to keep going in that direction.

Our souls are complex and within them we have constructed many roads that don't lead us to health and wholeness. From our early years our souls can be stunted, misshapen, and broken down by pain and evil. Our true voices become muted. As we understand this and lean into the Lord's ways, we can come out of denial and confusion and begin to build. Then spiritual formation takes place as each organ of our inner selves becomes like Christ. The Holy Spirit knows what he is about and keeps our growth moving forward even when it seems confusing or unorganized to us. We may see dimly now, but we are being transformed from "glory to glory" (2 Cor 3:18 NASB).

---

[13] J. I. Packer, *Knowing God* (Downers Grove, IL: InterVarsity Press, 1993), 41.

As Christ is formed in us, we become our true selves. This is the work of Christ's presence within. Payne wrote,

> The gifts of this Presence—the power to know, to say, to act—is ours, and we become the masterpiece of harmony God intended us to be. ... In union and communion with Him, our once fragmented souls are drawn together in one harmonious whole even as the pieces of a complex puzzle fall in place under the guidance of a masterful hand. We are no longer divided within.[14]

By his abundant sanctifying grace our souls can become masterpieces. Our true selves are no longer diminished and diluted by sin; we come truly alive, connected in every part. We are able to sing the song of our souls' transformation with true voices from every part drawn together in harmony.

Fr. Jacques Philippe wrote, "Only God is capable of creating totally unique masterpieces ... not according to our own ideas, but according to what God actually wants of us."[15] When we are governed by the Holy Spirit, he leads our faculties, senses, and desires, and we are inclined to his movements. His empowering presence gives us the capability to submit to him, to repent, and to receive his grace, so that everything in us thrives. Whatever parts of our true selves that were quelled now become freed, enhanced, and alive. We develop a solid perception of who we are, a deep sense of being and well-being. We become more able to love and respond to God and others.

In the chapters that follow we will discuss the different parts of our souls so that we can understand how we are supposed to function and what can go amiss. We can then ask the Lord for healing while learning to cultivate our wholeness.

---

[14] Leanne Payne, *The Broken Image* (originally published 1981, repr., Grand Rapids, MI: Hamewith Books, an Imprint of Baker Book House Company, 1996), 45.

[15] Philippe Jacques, *The School of the Holy Spirit* (n.p., Scepter Publishers Inc., 2007), 18–19. [For more information about Fr. Jacques Philippe's books, as well as speaking events, visit https://www.frjacquesphilippe.com.]

Prayer

Thank you, Lord, that as we begin this study of each part of the soul, we have the Holy Spirit who desires to resurrect everything within us. In your lovingkindness, put your finger on just those places within us that need change. Lord, you will reveal what hinders us while also revealing your glorious presence to heal.

It is such good news to our souls that everything we need you have provided and that your love is already ahead of us waiting to make a way for us to be transformed. We receive your love. Show us more and more how to believe it and receive it into every part of our souls. Thank you for the cross and the power of resurrection.

In the days to come, help us to see the capacity in every part of our souls and the need for healing. Give us the faith to believe you and receive all you are bringing to us. Enliven all that is within us by your indwelling presence. Build your home in us, Lord, make us your sanctuary, and let us collaborate with you in this construction. Expand our capacity to know you and be known by you that we might mature and thrive. Where we are disconnected within, bring unity. We want your fullness.

Highlight any areas where we need to forgive others, any persons from our past or present, so that we might free them and be freed ourselves. Uncover the judgments and misbeliefs that have been hidden within us, misdirecting our thoughts and motives.

We ask you to make us into the harmonious masterpieces you intend. We love you and commit our whole being—body, soul, and spirit, all you have created—into your hands. Work in us, re-form us, make us whole.

With our whole being, we trust your redemption. We thank you, Lord.

Homework

Begin to pray daily that the Holy Spirit would clarify areas of your soul that need healing, that he would uncover your misbeliefs and make you whole. Behold, he is making all things new! (Rv 21:5)

Recap

Our souls, all our inner powers and personhood, can be formed into the likeness of Christ by the power of the Holy Spirit as we invite him to transform every part of us. He knows all the complexities of our souls and can awaken every part of us. Even in our brokenness there is already a whole place within us where Christ dwells, and as we collaborate with him, we will see more and more wholeness emerge. He is making us into masterpieces of his grace.

In the chapters that follow we will discuss the different parts of our souls so that we can understand what can go amiss and how we are supposed to function, and so that we can ask the Lord for healing and learn to cultivate our wholeness.

Now let's take a look at the first section, Voices of Knowing and Choosing. We will discuss the transforming of the will, the rational mind, the receptive mind, and the conscience.

PART I

VOICES OF KNOWING AND CHOOSING

2

THE WILL

The will is the capacity within our souls to choose, resolve, initiate, decide, and stand in our decisions. Its voice is *I choose, I decide, I determine*, and in using this voice we make choices—sometimes small, sometimes powerful—that help us grow and mature and set our direction. The will encompasses the whole soul working together, with all its branches and capacities, and is truly remarkable.

Willard, in *Renovation of the Heart*, describes the function of this faculty as "to originate or refrain from originating something"; to give "consents" and "non-consents" (our real yes or no); to give us dignity (unless we use it to get our own way, thus enslaving us to the self); and to enable the capacity for self-determination, which is the capacity to be and to do.[16] The will is vital in our development as persons. We want our wills to be alive, healthy, strong, and active. God has given us the capacity to make choice after choice, and to direct our own thoughts and lives. This human freedom to choose where we focus our minds determines all other freedoms.

We not only have the capacity and the freedom of determination, but we also have the authority to make our own choices. When we act as if we have no choice, we are in a victim mode. If we believe we are powerless and without choice, we will end up reacting, usually with either passivity or aggression, instead of rising to choose. What action we choose and where we place our thoughts really is our own choice—whether we build the true

---

[16] Willard, *Renovation of the Heart*, 144.

and the good or whether we choose foolishness and evil. More than we realize, we really are in charge of our choices and what we create by them.

The will is essential in building and rebuilding our souls as we abide in Christ. Payne wrote in *The Broken Image*, "As we will to be *in* him, he gathers together the scattered parts of ourselves we have been separated from."[17] He gathers, he integrates, and he builds. Thus, with our wills we choose to abide in him and let him do his healing work in us.

The will is essential to our well-being and vitality in Christ, to walking in holiness, and to resisting sin. Choices build habits and habits build character. Choices help us to become established in Christ: steadfast, stable, and mature (Col 1:23; 2:5–7). A lifetime of growth in maturity comes from our choices. With choice after choice, we become firmer and surer, emerging as victorious, confident people who have developed nobility of character. So, it is imperative that we understand the centrality and function of the will.

The will is the organizing center of personality that gives us the capacity to develop a true self, who we are really designed to be.[18] It requires agreement or disagreement followed by action. The will is the active authority that should be in charge of what our minds think about, of what appetites we act from, of what pictures we allow our imaginations to dwell on, of what boundaries and intensity we allow our emotions. This is because the will is responsible for ordering all other capacities of the soul. When our wills are strong, healthy, and active we can fulfill the desires of our hearts, keep our appetites in check, govern our emotions, listen to our conscience, pay attention to our intuitions, decide where to set our thoughts, and form godly characters. It is with the will that we choose faith, hope, love, and all the characteristics and fruits of the Spirit.

In *Ourselves,*[19] Charlotte Mason gives us a helpful metaphor for the will, describing it as the prime minister within the government of the soul. The prime minister takes responsibility *for* the executive branch of government and is answerable *to* the king. That image captures the essence of the will, which is to govern our souls and bodies while submitted to the

---

[17] Payne, *The Broken Image*, 124.

[18] Pertuit, lecture at the School of Pastoral Care Ministries.

[19] Charlotte Mason, *Ourselves* (Hoboken, N.J.: Start Publishing LLC, 2012), e-book, location 324.

King of Kings. As Payne writes of the essential nature of our wills: "The will is that in man which chooses whether to be or not to be."[20] We choose the sanctification of becoming who we truly are in Christ or whether we fail to grow and become. The first and greatest act of our wills is to choose Christ, to receive his sacrifice at the cross, and to give him the place of lordship. This enables our "becoming."

Pause and Reflect

What has been your understanding of the will? How did you frame it? As you read this description of the will, did you realize how powerful, profound, and central the place of the will is within the soul? Is there a sentence or idea that struck you as most important? Has your understanding shifted in some way?

Relationship to Emotions

In a church age where emotions are sometimes overemphasized, we need to shift our emphasis to faith. We are not designed to live out of our emotions as a source, therefore we must learn to live out of the will. Often people act from their feelings because that seems so natural, but then are left at the mercy of those feelings. In our spiritual formation we need to confront this tendency to live from feelings and learn to live from our wills.[21]

To move forward in our maturity, we must take responsibility to recognize and acknowledge our emotions, and then to make righteous choices from our wills. F. B Meyer wrote, "We have no direct control over our feelings, but we have over our will. Our wills are ours, to make them God's. God does not hold us responsible for what we feel, but for what we will. In his sight we're not what we feel, but what we will. Let us, therefore, not live in the summerhouse of emotion, but in the central citadel of the will, wholly yielded and devoted to the will of God."[22] Our emotional states are not the test of our spiritual states; our choices are. We decide what we live from.

---

[20] Leanne Payne, *Crisis in Masculinity* (Grand Rapids, MI: Baker Books, 1985), 79.

[21] Willard, *Renovation of the Heart*, 35.

[22] F. B. Meyer, *The Secret of Guidance* (Hoboken, NJ: Start Publishing LLC, 2012), 12–13.

Corrie ten Boom in *Tramp for the Lord* describes her experience speaking at a church after the end of World War II. A prison guard from the concentration camp where she had been interred heard her and afterward came up and asked her to forgive him, extending his hand. Remembering the horror of that place, she recognized him and felt she simply could not forgive. "And still I stood there with the coldness clutching my heart. But forgiveness is not an emotion—I knew that too. Forgiveness is an act of the will, and the will can function regardless of the temperature of the heart [emotions]. 'Jesus, help me!' I prayed silently. 'I can lift my hand. I can do that much. You supply the feeling.'"[23] As she lifted her hand to shake his, love flooded in. She writes of the same incident again in *The Hiding Place*, commenting, "When He tells us to love our enemies, He gives, along with the command, the love itself."[24] Regardless of the "temperature of the heart," we can choose the next right thing.

One encounter with the Lord can change us. We need these encounters and our encounters with the Lord may be filled with significant emotion while he is depositing something substantive within us. But we must continue with what he has deposited, even after the initial emotions have faded, persevering in faith and obedience until our obedience is joyfully concurring with God's will. Growth follows obedience as we cultivate the new things he has deposited. Our dispositions and inclinations begin to be transformed as new grooves are made in our character. What had been hard before now becomes a welcome part of us.

We may feel disobedience is inevitable because obedience seems optional. Indeed, God gives us a choice. But we're truly designed for obedience—by creation and by resurrection grace. By engaging our wills, we can still obey, regardless of the emotions and circumstances.

Pause and Reflect

Have you confused your emotions with the will or overemphasized the place of emotions? Ask the Lord to teach you how to live from your will and not from your emotions. What might that look like for you?

---

[23] Corrie ten Boom, *Tramp for the Lord* (Grand Rapids, MI: Revell, 1974), 56.

[24] Corrie ten Boom, *The Hiding Place* (Washington Depot, CT: Chosen Books, 1971), 215.

Development of the Will

How does the capacity of the will develop? Formation of the will begins in childhood; to help a child develop his will, parents must nurture this. Parents are responsible to form character, foster the will, and develop good habits in their children. By age two, children have their own voice, perspective, and ability to think independently (and to say no!). My youngest grandson is two years old now and he bosses around the large tolerant family dog (really any dog available) practicing his "no" and "sit" commands. Usually the dog just walks on by, but this toddler doesn't give up. He's practicing. At my house, he nods his head yes while saying no when he's doing something he should not. It's adorable in a little one, but someday he will have to learn to say a real yes or no and live with larger consequences.

Some parents feel threatened by their children's emerging wills, or feel they should control their children into obedience, and so crush or subvert a child's emerging independence with harsh discipline. Instead, parents need to let children truly feel and name their own feelings while cultivating obedience.

As our wills are formed by external nurture and instruction, we can slowly internalize good discipline. We can gradually replace the compliance that comes from fear of punishment or desire for reward, with loving obedience, in which we want to please the one who asked and that is the reward. We pass from extrinsic to intrinsic motivation. No one has to tell me any longer; now I internally know and choose. By this, my will is strengthened in good ways.

But sometimes we are dominated by our parents, or are left to fend for ourselves, and so we can develop weak and uncertain wills or become self-willed. If we have been raised by a hard father or mother, or even influenced by someone like a dominant grandparent, pastor, or coach, we may need a freeing and healing of the will. We have to come up out of compliance from fear of punishment and into our own personhood, our own choices.

As an adult, if we can't become appropriately angry, if we don't know how to say no, we are inadvertently inviting others to manipulate or abuse us—they intuit that they can take advantage of us. We can even give up on spiritual things that require effort because our wills are weak. This is deadly to our spiritual formation. One of the false voices of the will is the compliance of *I don't know; you choose for me.* The other false voice is the stubborn, self-willed *I demand my own way.* Both come from broken places.

Early in my Christian life I had no idea what boundaries were about or that I could even have them. I was raised in a military home by good and moral parents, but I was not allowed to express much of my own will or boundaries. Compliance was expected and noncompliance quickly punished. I didn't know how to separate myself from the internalized will of my father or to form boundaries where I actually took responsibility for my own life and kept out the things that shouldn't be there. I became a committed Christian at age twenty-one, but my own will was just beginning to form rightly. For many years, I had significant confusion surrounding my will, and a keen sense of shame.

Confusion surrounding the will is commonly found in adults who were hurt when they were younger but were not old enough to understand what was happening. We often don't know what ought to be normal and may feel: *Someone else is living my life for me, making my decisions.* We allow others to choose and decide for us: "Tell me what I should do." We haven't found our own voices or discovered what we really wanted and expressed it in healthy ways. Sadly, some people go through their whole lives without exercising much of their will. Even with the Lord, we can sometimes live under the assumption that he is in control, and we have no choice. Not true! We partner with him as he is at work within us (Phil 2:12–13). He never puppets or controls us but invites us to walk with him as our lives unfold.

Where our wills have been bound—sometimes almost extinguished— through another's dominance, or through our own passivity (or some combination of these), we need the presence of the Lord to heal and release us. We may have only had the will of another "commanding" us. We need deliverance, especially women (but also men) who have become passive in relationships with others who are controlling them. In this case, we must confess the passivity of allowing someone other than the Lord Jesus to have dominion. We repent of our idolatry to that person and any territory we have given up to them.[25]

---

[25] Carla Waterman, lecture series, "Capacities and Motions of the Soul," given at Church of the Resurrection, Wheaton, IL, 1999.

Pause and Reflect

Reflect on your childhood. Who or what helped your will develop in good ways? What specifically can you see that was lacking in that development?

In what ways were you treated that crushed or stifled the good development of your will? Did you turn toward passivity of will, or toward stubborn self-will, or a combination of these?

Where do you need to ask forgiveness, to forgive others, or to forgive yourself? Invite the Lord into that process now.

Surrender

How can our wills be both strong and surrendered to the Lord? The highest, holiest use of our wills is choosing the way of the Lord. Surrender ought to be robust and active, not passive; to surrender to his lordship takes strength of will. We don't give up our wills so that we no longer bear responsibility for our choices. Instead, we unite ours with his in surrender, and we yield to his greater way where necessary. Our transformation is not only up to God; it's up to us to join our wills to his as he does the work. We trust him and partner collaboratively with him.

We tend to swing between the passivity of "the responsibility is all God's" and the teeth-gritting striving of "the responsibility is all mine." We aren't supposed to live either way—whether in the path of least resistance or in the strain of self-effort that negates grace.

Passivity is the absence of purpose and resolve within us that makes it difficult for us to believe that purpose and resolution exist in God, and therefore are to exist in us. We can stay with passive, unexamined reactions, or develop good habits. As we develop good habits, at first the thing (such as an exercise program or a daily time with the Lord or refusing to overspend) is a conscious, perhaps difficult, choice. But as we repeatedly choose the new habit, it becomes as easy and natural as an unexamined, effortless reaction. We first have to choose to make the good happen, and then it becomes a part of us. Habit replaces habit, and as good habits are set in, we begin to respond more automatically.[26]

To choose what is right is a collaboration of our wills and God's strengthening (Phil 2:13). It is an active choice, but not one of striving. God does for us what we cannot do, but he will not do what we can choose for ourselves. By his grace, he even helps us choose for ourselves. Our hearts say, *I choose, I walk forward, but I can't do it without your empowering strength*, and he answers us in our need. Then, like Corrie ten Boom, we don't wait for the feeling to spur us on, we simply lift our hands and choose to do the next right thing.

François Fénelon wrote, "All that lies in your power is the direction of your will. Give that up to God without reservation. The important question is … whether you desire whatever God wills."[27] Before surrender, there may be a certain uneasiness until we have settled the question of whether we desire God's will, whether we say, "not my will but yours." But once we choose his will, he gives us the power and freedom to choose what is best, what is most genuine. And in choosing his will we find our true identities more and more.

Pause and Reflect

Have you deeply surrendered your will to the Lord, uniting yourself to his will? If you have, what was that like? If not, are you willing to do that now? Or, perhaps, might you need to reaffirm your yes to him?

Have you ever found yourself in a position of being willing but not able to carry through? Why do you think that may have happened? Reflect on what degree to which you may have been striving versus leaning into God's enabling power.

---

[26] Waterman, "Capacities and Motions of the Soul."

[27] François Fénelon, *Let Go* (Amberson, PA: Scroll Publishing Co., 2007), 9.

Perseverance

The will helps us stay with difficult tasks and stay present in painful circumstances, not striving, but trusting. I used to walk in a lovely park near my home and would mix the walking with some jogging. When I was first diagnosed with cancer in the spring of 2007, I was out for a walk and sensed an internal spurring (often how I experience the Holy Spirit) to run for a bit. I thought I would just run to the bridge ahead of me and cross it, but after I reached it, I noticed a bench farther ahead and thought perhaps I could run a bit more, even though I wasn't completely fit for it. I was getting winded, but I noticed a sign ahead and continued running toward it. I kept going on the path in this way for a good while, one small goal to the next, and was surprised at how far I eventually ran. Afterward, I realized I was being prepared to face the next daunting year of chemotherapy and surgeries. I could look to the one next thing ahead, fixing my eyes on that as a goal, and keep going. There would be strength enough for that. And to just keep going, taking the next necessary step, was victory.

At the very moment you feel most inadequate to obey, if you will step forward anyway, you will find that what meets you is God's strength to take the next step. God meets us right there. We receive strength for the very moment we are taking that step. Surrender to the Lord in this way is not passive, but a clear, strong choice. It's when we are leaning on him that we are strong. His Spirit is animating our wills.

The Russian poet Irina Ratushinskaya, a Christian dissident imprisoned for critiquing the Soviet regime, wrote *Grey Is the Color of Hope*. In it, she called her will her "royal" will when she dissented with dignity.[28] In her subsequent book, *In The Beginning*, she wrote that our lives are like training grounds run by a coach who wants us to pursue our full potential. When we're tempted to slack off, the coach pushes, prods, and encourages us on. Knowing what will make us stronger and surer, the coach does not relent in his expectations.[29] This is a great example of

---

[28] Irina Ratushinskaya, *Grey Is the Color of Hope*, trans. Alyona Kojevnikov (New York: Alfred A. Knopf, 1988), 9.

[29] Irina Ratushinskaya, *In the Beginning*, trans. Alyona Kojevnikov (New York: Alfred A. Knopf, 1991), 28.

choosing to move forward even when we feel it's too much. The Lord shows us that it's not too much, that we really can obey. The will is like a muscle that gets stronger the more we obey. We realize we can choose things we could never choose before.

Pause and Reflect

Can you recall a time when you thought a difficult task or painful circumstance was "just too much?" Were you able to step forward in trust and surrender? What made the difference?

Was there a time when you did not choose to surrender to the Lord, disciplining yourself to obey and trust? Have you asked his forgiveness? Do that now, and once again surrender to his ways. We can always begin anew.

By perseverance we take possession of our own souls. For example, Paul wrote in Colossians 3:15, "Let the peace of Christ rule in your hearts" (NIV). We can stay in our anxiety, or we can be responsible in our obedience to God's Word. We can say, "I will not let my heart be troubled, but I choose to let your peace rule in my heart." That's taking possession of our own souls.

When we endure difficult times, looking to our good Father, we find that our discipline develops into greater perseverance and self-governing. Our resolve strengthens to continue on the path of holiness, and we become clearer about our own hearts and what God is about in us. Payne wrote,

> It is when man is obedient, when he wills to unite himself with God, that he finds himself to be one person—a person whose choices are continually changing him from the very center of his being into that perfected person that shall be. Such a person's will is magnificently free. … Such a person's will is vibrantly alive and active … infused by the very power of God.[30]

---

[30] Payne, *Crisis in Masculinity*, 81.

Our freedom comes when the will is focused wholly on God. The only real freedom is when our wills are bound to his in an undivided way (see Ps 86:11). We are no longer double-minded and unstable, ruled by our own impulses, appetites, or emotions. We no longer let our thoughts and attitudes be set by reactions to others or to circumstances. Instead, we choose our attitudes.

Psychologists can help us understand how our environments or our pasts have shaped us. They can explain how we have become who we are, but we also need a hopeful vision for what we can become. God has a vision for what we are to become—and we have the deciding vote whether or not to pursue that vision. That is why sin weakens the will, brings it under dominion, and chokes it. It keeps us from spiritual formation. But a strong, healthy will enables us to pursue the Lord and set our attitudes and thoughts on good things. For instance, when we are tempted, we can learn to change our thoughts by setting them on something else. If we have an idea that is struggling for entrance and it is a wrong idea, we can fight it by replacing it with something else. This is why we need the Word of God in us!

We don't need to worry so much about extinguishing negative thoughts. Instead, we build the true and the good. Ten Boom told another story in *The Hiding Place* that illustrates this. When she and her sister Betsy were in Ravensbrück concentration camp, it was filthy, crowded, and full of fleas. Betsy, looking up toward the Lord instead of down in self-pity, focused on what the Lord wanted. She asked the Lord to show them how to live in such a terrible place. She didn't sink into easy misery but instead chose to thank the Lord for the place, even for the fleas. The sisters later realized why they had complete freedom to pray and hold Bible studies for the desperate women there: the soldiers wouldn't enter the dorm because of the fleas![31] The point was not the fleas, but rather the choice of being thankful in that circumstance versus being full of self-pity. The battle was won right there, in that choice, and in the actions that followed.

Where we place our minds is the issue at the heart of biblical psychology. A thought comes to us, a temptation, and our conscience may not stop it. When the conscience abdicates, the will has to make a choice. The conscience may warn us, but our wills cast the deciding vote

---

[31] Ten Boom, *The Hiding Place*, 180.

to let something in to our minds and imaginations or to close the gates to the enemy. Isaiah 28:6 says the Lord will give "strength to those who turn back the battle at the gate" (NIV).

Let's pray for the healing and strengthening of the will. As the prime minister of the soul, it is so important for our wills to be free and strong!

Prayer for Healing and Strengthening the Will

Lord, if my will has been bound, cramped, or nearly extinguished by another through their dominance or inattention, please show me. Enable me to forgive anyone who has crushed my will, who has taken away my right to choose or my voice to speak. Enable me to forgive anyone who should have helped me develop a strong, healthy will but did not. I acknowledge that this was neglect and a lack of care.

Lord, you want no one else commanding me or demanding that I do their will. Show me, Lord, where I have bent in toward another and let that person dominate me. Show me any place where I have been passive and have abdicated my will. Reveal any sinful dependency on persons or things, any way I have demanded from others the identity I can gain only from you, Lord. Reveal anything I have attempted to find my worth in apart from you.

Lord, forgive me where I have abdicated my will, been passive and hidden, or believed that I didn't have the strength in you or the right to choose well. Forgive me for not using or for misusing my will, for any wrong forms of submission or codependency toward another person. I renounce my idolatry in Jesus's name. *With the eyes of your heart, imagine yourself bent toward that person, then straightening up from that position.*

Lord, I thank you for your forgiveness; I receive it.

Lord, heal and free me. Unbind and untangle me from the will and control of any other. Release me from the hold of evil dominance or the immaturity of another. Untangle my will that I might know the difference between my own will and that of another. Give me discernment and understanding in this. Set me free!

Where there is confusion or duplicity, cleanse and heal me. Where there is atrophy, bring my will to life by your Spirit and unite everything within me to be able to choose. Release me from all crippling and disapproving influences. Release my voice and my gifts. May I know more what it means to be filled with your will and to know the real authority I have. Though my will is insufficient, I am yours and you strengthen my will. I choose to make my will one with yours.

Now tell the Lord that you choose life, creativity, initiation, maturity, your own yes and no. Pray this prayer of St. Augustine: "Descend into me, divine, masculine, eternal Will, descend into me, radiate up through me. Lord, command what Thou wilt, then will what Thou commandest."[32]

Lord, thank you that my will surrendered to you is a strong will because even in my weakness I am joined to you. I ask you to meet me in the journey of choosing well, of learning to function with a healthy will, and of learning to be strengthened by your grace.

Homework

Several times a day stop and give your will to God; tell him you yield to his will.

Recap

The will, the organizing center of the personality, is essential to our vitality. The will is responsible for ordering all the other capacities of the soul. As we exercise our wills to choose, we are able to develop our true voices. Now let's turn from our ways of choosing to look at our ways of knowing.

---

[32] Quoted in Payne, *The Healing Presence,* 74.

3

THE RATIONAL MIND

The body of Christ has sometimes devalued the intellect, but God created each of us with good rational minds. He is extremely interested in our thoughts and our thought processes: "You have searched me, LORD, and you know me. … You perceive my thoughts from afar. … You are familiar with all my ways" (Ps 139:1–4 NIV). He knows all our thoughts while giving us the freedom to choose where we focus our thoughts. When we come to grow in Christ, we begin to realize the importance of our thoughts and recognize our vital responsibility to have renewed minds in him.

As Willard wrote,

> Thoughts are the place where we can and must begin to change. There, the light of God first begins to move upon us through the Word of Christ, and there the divine Spirit begins to direct our will. … The ultimate freedom we have as human beings is the power to select what we will allow or require our minds to dwell upon.[33]

No one can take this ultimate freedom from us.

Often we don't realize how automatic and patterned our thoughts have become. They are informed and created by even deeper patterns of beliefs. We have taken in knowledge, experiences, beliefs, memories, and attitudes, all of which inform our core beliefs. Those core beliefs are then compressed and reinforced to create a value system which orients us to distinct patterns

---

[33] Willard, *Renovation of the Heart*, 95.

of thought. Our beliefs inspire our thoughts. Whatever we believe at our core spills out in our thoughts, words, feelings, and actions, and forms our characters, eventually determining our destinies. The good news is that we can change our thoughts by interrupting and replacing them, eventually transforming our thought lives and our deeper beliefs.

The true voice of the intellect is: *I consider, reflect, perceive, and judge with understanding and truth.* The false voices are: *I'm darkened and compulsive in my thoughts and unable or unwilling to choose what I set my mind on;* or *I'm confused in my thoughts and beliefs.* In the false voices, we have become paralyzed into one way of thinking, or we have abdicated responsibility for what we think and believe.

The rational mind, functioning with connections to the receptive mind, forms channels for thoughts to run in. Consistently healthy thoughts undergird and build good neurological channels in the brain. Our power of thought is so great. We have the capacity to dwell on what is true, honorable, pure, lovely, and excellent (Phil 4:8), and to create these good neurological channels. When we take responsibility for how and where we set our minds, the Spirit can fill us with life-giving thoughts and peace (Rom 8:6) and, while managing our emotions and developing our characters, we build sound neural networks.

Strongholds

In 2 Corinthians 10:3–5 we are exhorted to pull down strongholds and bring our thoughts into obedience to Christ. Physical strongholds are well-fortified refuges with sturdy stone walls. In an unhealthy spiritual stronghold, we can think of the stones as thought patterns in conflict with God—our ideas, ideals, reasonings, and imaginations that seem reasonable or even right to us, but which the demonic can inhabit and hide behind. (See 1 Pt 5:8–9; Eph 6:12).

We need to recognize the truth of Galatians 5:9 (TPT): "Don't you know that when you allow even a little lie into your heart, it can permeate your entire belief system?" The trouble really is with what we believe and keep believing, what we think and keep thinking. This is why we must learn to tear down strongholds and bring our thoughts under the lordship of Christ. As we convert our thoughts, we convert our souls.

Our defensive reactions to life can build a whole diseased complex of core beliefs that becomes our default. It's not so much about the things that have happened to us as it is the lies and misbeliefs that we have taken in or formed from those things. These lies tend to center around shame, hopelessness, powerlessness, confusion, fear, abandonment, and invalidation.

In my counseling I have seen these patterns countless times. Often people who were shamed in childhood as a form of discipline learned to internalize that shame and now shame themselves for making mistakes or not living up to a certain standard. Others who were not empowered to learn to make their own decisions feel uncertain, powerless, confused, and alone when they face decisions as adults.

Strongholds are like command centers with well-developed means of protecting and coping. They can spring up in any area of wounding or sin when we follow our own reasoning. For example, if we have a stronghold of dread, it will inform our thoughts and emotions with a negative expectancy. Then we are not free to delight continually in the Lord and live in joy and peace. We need to ask the Lord to reveal the strongholds in our thinking, strongholds of which we are many times unaware.

I have often seen people who are suffering from a stronghold of abandonment and invalidation who do not realize that they have a coping style that perpetuates their pain. That coping style originated with childhood rejection, invalidation, or lack of affirmation and nurture.

Childhood Messages

Old, deeply embedded messages that were planted in childhood come up unbidden in pervasive and cyclical ways to rapidly inform us how to feel and think. When we believe a lie, we are lending our hearts to it to create our future stories. Our hearts repeatedly recreate this lie, continuing to influence our destinies. It feels so true to us that it keeps us bound. We operate under the wrong premises, feel darkened emotions, work with skewed perceptions, and make decisions accordingly.

During our childhood years we learn to live with certain messages that develop into mental and emotional strongholds with power to control us. These create lifestyle responses that set themselves against the promises of God. While wounds may be forgotten by the conscious, present mind, they are still stored away. Old pain then covers over our true identity—who we are created to be. This is especially true when trauma is part of our stories.

Core messages can develop into strongholds, patterns that attract and comfort us because they are familiar and automatic, yet also hinder us. Some examples of such patterns are:

- confusion, uncertainty, and indecisiveness;
- emotional reactivity;
- difficulty resolving interpersonal conflict;
- poor self-image, self-doubt, and self-criticism;
- control issues;
- codependency;
- addictions;
- depression and hopelessness;
- shame;
- a sense of powerlessness;
- anxiety and fear; and
- self-focused introspection.

Pattern of Formation: The Unhealed Heart

This graphic depicts the development of the unhealed heart formed via a cyclical process in which our faulty beliefs, thoughts, emotions, character, and choices interact.

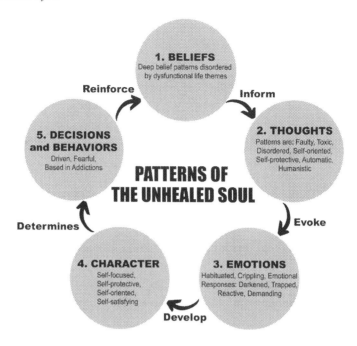

In this diagram the cycle begins with the deep core beliefs that form in childhood from experiences, pain, and deficits. When we are wounded, our wounds are delivered with a toxic message (spoken or unspoken) about our identity, value, worth, appearance, safety, performance, power, gender, and other intrinsic and acquired characteristics, attributes, and qualities. These embedded messages inform thoughts that become patterns of disordered thinking (strongholds). The dark thought patterns, aided by demonic forces, evoke emotions that disrupt peace and joy in our lives. These dark thoughts and emotions then define and dictate our lives.[34] Our character forms because of the thoughts, emotions, and decisions that come from these thoughts and emotions. And the cycle continues, reinforcing our deep beliefs.

Our core beliefs may have their origin in messages passed down generationally in our families. These beliefs may contain toxic ideas such as:

- "We don't discuss family matters with outsiders; that is disloyal."
- "I'm dirty because I was violated."

---

[34] See Therapon Institute, *Spirit, Soul, and Body: A Total Approach to Recovery for Hurting and Healing People* (Crockett, TX: Therapon Institute, n.d.).

- "Unless someone else tells me what to do, I'll be overwhelmed."
- "If I don't perform well, I won't be loved and acceptable."
- "If I allow myself to really feel my emotions, they will be dangerous and unmanageable, and I will go crazy."
- "It's not all right to be angry."
- "If you don't approve of me, I feel unworthy and shamed."

Where we have been wounded in the early years, messages attached to the wounds create a life script. These messages have formed and distorted our core beliefs. They set up a kind of algorithm within us, telling us how to feel and what rules to follow in the future. For instance, if I have had experiences of deep friendships with women, I might meet someone new with positive expectations and an open heart. But if my relationships have been littered with betrayal or rejection in the past, I might approach a new acquaintance in a self-protective way because I am transferring my old pain into the present.

Our past shapes our future unless it is interrupted with truth. It takes deliberate effort to examine how we are feeling, thinking, and acting, and the deeper core beliefs. We must be willing not only to change as a person, but also to revise our old stories as truth becomes clearer. We edit one insight at a time, letting the truth in. Our souls are designed for growth, but we can only grow when we take responsibility for our attitudes and thoughts. Then our narratives begin to change as we take in truth. It will help if we see the change process as a privilege—as part of governing our own souls.

Pause and Reflect

In any area of your thoughts, perhaps in topics mentioned above—shame, hopelessness, powerlessness, confusion, fear, abandonment, and invalidation—can you recognize the places of automatic default?

Ask the Holy Spirit to help you identify darkened thought patterns and specific lies you have believed as if they are true.

List them in your journal then invite the Lord to tell you his truth to replace the lies. (The journaling exercise at the end of this chapter gives you helpful steps to follow.)

Rumination

We have been discussing the rational mind, and how healthy thinking often gets hijacked by strongholds consisting of distorted beliefs. These strongholds are perpetuated by introspective rumination. Let's take a look at how rumination shapes the rational mind and perpetuates the patterns of the unhealed soul. Then we will return and contrast the cycle of the development of the unhealed soul with that of the transformed soul.

While meditation on the living word is a powerful habit that aids in renewing our minds, the wrong kind of rumination is a seriously debilitating habit of mind. Unhealthy rumination or introspection is the habit of inward self-examination that involves the rational mind as well as the imagination, intuition, emotions, desires, and will. We are constantly preoccupied in our minds, rethinking the past, looking within ourselves for answers, imagining how things could have been different. Or we are anxiously projecting into an imagined future. Such rumination is isolating, seductive, and dangerous, and can develop into a stronghold, a command center where the demonic can hide.[35]

Introspection can be relentless in self-criticism as we examine ourselves through the lens of either self-reproach or self-approval, vacillating between the two. This can cause us to tear the past apart, deconstructing but never restructuring into a meaningful whole. In counseling I have seen some of the damaging outcomes of rumination and the surprise when people realize that their own introspections are causing such damage. People steeped in introspection struggle with guilt, shame, regret, fear of the future, indecision, and a fixation on the self.

Our own intellect is attempting to somehow reshape the past or control future outcomes and in doing so we can be consumed by negative thoughts and regret. This is never from the Holy Spirit and produces a distorted

---

[35] Payne, *The Healing Presence*, 186.

picture because it is highly subjective and prevents the light of his truth from entering.

Underlying these patterns of thought is a deeper anxiety and unrest, an unsettled state in which we may constantly feel something is wrong with us. We are mired in our introspections, apart from his presence, yet afraid to stop thinking. Ruminating on solutions and what ifs becomes a toxic alternative to experiencing and dealing with our anxiety in healthy ways.

Rumination is an endless dialogue with ourselves, and is far from what God has designed us for. We were created to interact with God and with others, and to take in beauty and truth. When we function in these intended ways, the movement within us is up and out and open, receptive to what is good and other than us.

In contrast, introspection is a down-and-in movement, closed. It's like a closed circuit, which is an unhealthy system because nothing new and fresh is coming in. It just loops and loops back into itself with no fresh outside input. Lewis described this madness: "… Your thoughts merely go round and round a wearisome circle, now hopeful, now despondent, then hopeful again—that way madness lies."[36]

Introspection is a madness that causes us to look hard into ourselves for solutions. It is an idolatry that puts self on the throne as the arbiter of truth. We have chosen to think about the self rather than be present to what we are really feeling and experiencing; we have chosen to manage rather than to suffer with the genuine issues of life and bring them to the Lord.

Like all idols, introspection is a destroyer and invites darkness and torment. Sadly, it keeps us in a place of estrangement from our own hearts and we live a kind of provisional existence. Only God knows what is in our darkness (Dn 2:22) and only in him does light dwell. Our darkness is no surprise to him, and is no obstacle to his light if we let him in.

Avoiding Shame and Anxiety

Introspection leads to discouragement, shame, regret, and depression. It destroys our joy and peace. So, why do we do it? One reason is that

---

[36] Walter Hooper, ed., *Collected Letters of C. S. Lewis, Vol. 1*, (San Francisco: HarperSanFrancisco, 2004), 924.

we are trying to reduce shame. From childhood, we may have had so much punishment, so much shame, that we are now shaming ourselves, being self-critical and trying to find a way out of that shame. We turn on ourselves: "Why did you do that? What were you thinking?" We reason: "If I fix myself, if I figure it out, I won't be punished." We try to reduce our sense of the shame that drives introspection. But this only avoids reality.

What is the real antidote to fear and shame? Love, always love. 1 John 4:18 tells us God's perfect love is the antidote to fear because fear is about *hiding* from punishment, and we no longer need to hide. Christ has suffered our punishment, and we need no longer fear because he has accepted us and declared us righteous.

Introspection is also our attempt to avoid anxiety. Anxiety propels the scrutiny of introspection. We are attempting to gain a more secure future and avoid the pain of the past and so tamp down our anxiety. But this is exhausting and painful, keeping us constantly thinking in circles, the way of "madness" Lewis described. We aren't able to live fully in the present.

God's process is different. We are not to continually scrutinize and relive. We are to take what is of value and leave the rest, resisting regret. Living by faith and listening to his life-giving words, we trust him to speak to us, to sort out our messes, and to "work all things together for good." In this way, we don't squander the present.

Pause and Reflect

How much of your life do you really experience firsthand and in the present? And how much do you default into the past or future by introspection? For instance, have you lived alive today to the present moment, to others, and to the Lord?

Introspection: What Can We Do About It?

Sadly, we can mistake introspection for real maturity. Healthy self-examination involves the Holy Spirit, asking him to illumine what is true and real. When we ask him, rather than asking the self, he will deal with the real root of an issue and bring us to truth and freedom. As we rejoice in truth, we can learn to love others, God, nature, beauty, and our true selves. Also, we can listen to the Lord and be drawn deeply into the presence of Christ.

Where we have participated in our own enslavement, we can choose the process of freedom. To come free, we face a significant, life-changing decision. We must decide that we are not going to keep managing the past or securing the future. Instead, we will live now, in Christ.

The Lord is inviting us to trust him and dethrone our idolatrous ways of thinking. We can begin with repentance, turning away from trusting ourselves as a way not to be present to the felt pain, especially the pain of powerlessness in the early years of life. We abandon self-protection and soundly renounce the idol-god self because we have narcissistically worshipped our own realities. As we repent of the practice of introspection, we decide we are going to enter the battle to overcome it. We start "… fitting every loose thought and emotion and impulse into the structure of life shaped by Christ … clearing the ground of every obstruction and building lives of obedience into maturity" (2 Cor 10:5–6 MSG).[37]

We must come out of ruminating and into believing. Called to a life of faith, to walk in the Spirit, we learn to practice his presence and listen to him. We must choose truth over and over to cultivate new habits of thought and practice. We will face battles to regain lost ground in our souls, but his empowering grace will meet us in each of these battles, strengthening us.

Our greatest weapon is renewing the mind with truth. We can pray: "Thank you for your presence now, Lord. I choose to bring these thoughts captive to Christ. I choose to be present here and now and to look outward to you. I step out of introspection and into the light."

In doing this, we are using our wills to direct the rational mind back to its beneficial use and as a result our hearts can be flooded with light. Then it often helps to move our physical body and to go and do something simple and practical, focusing outward on a task. But we also recognize that we are going to need to deal with the core issues causing our anxieties even as we choose to transform this habit.

---

[37] Adapted from Payne, lecture on *Listening Prayer.*

Transformation

Now, let's discuss how we can collaborate with the Lord in the transformation of the patterns of our unhealed souls into patterns of wholeness. The mind will be our close companion our whole life and it can be our ally or our tormentor. We can wonderfully make it our ally. Because God is our redeemer, we have the power of agreement, of aligning our thoughts with God's truth and rejecting painful messages from the past, which gives life and power to our thoughts. We find good news in 2 Corinthians 10:4, which says we have weapons with "divine power to demolish strongholds"!

The way we go about demolishing strongholds is important. Christ came to set us free from the chains of sin and negative habits, and the wonderful news is that by the grace of his empowering presence and our responsive discipline, we can establish new thought patterns. As we say no to lie-based thinking, we can say yes to the truth, receiving it and believing it. As each no and yes develops, new habits follow. These are not broad choices, but very specific ones. For example, when tempted to pick apart our inadequacies we choose instead to turn our thoughts to gratefulness for the gifts and abilities the Lord has given us. Choice after choice, we watch over our heart-thoughts (see Prv 4:23).

Sometimes we have been so invested in our misbeliefs that it is scary to consider what it will cost to give up the lies and to live in freedom. Therefore, we can't just focus on finding the lie and removing it. Scripture says we are to "take captive every thought to make it obedient to Christ" (2 Cor 10:5 NIV).

As the lie is uprooted, it is replaced with truth and trust in Christ. We turn around the negative thought and replace it, exchanging it for truth. For example, if I am feeling shameful thoughts of self-hatred, I can choose to banish those thoughts and show courtesy and compassion to myself as the Lord does, inviting him into that.

As an illustration of this in my own life, when I am beginning to experience a downward cycle with thoughts of shame, fear, unworthiness, or hopelessness, I arrest those thoughts, simultaneously looking to the Lord and renewing my mind. I replace my thoughts by saying aloud: "Lord, I'm coming *back*." When I say that, I am taking in the truths of my belovedness. "Back" is my shorthand for:

B –   beloved (Col 3:12; Eph 1:6)
A –   accepted (Eph 1:6; Rom 15:7)
C –   chosen, complete, and called (Eph 1:4, 11–12; I Pt 1:1; Col 2:10)
K –   kept (I Pt 1:5) and known (Ps 139:1; I Cor 13:12)

Then I meditate for a few moments on how beloved, accepted, chosen, kept and known I really am as his presence abides in me. Continuing this over the years, I have cultivated a new freedom with greater ease and peace of heart. I return to this again and again as part of the renewal process I will discuss next.

As our minds are renewed, we grow to have the very mind of Christ. His Spirit lives within us, which far transcends our limited understanding and intelligence. In fact, because we have received the Spirit, we now can freely know the things God gives us with spiritual thoughts and words (1 Cor 2:6–16). As a result, we can reason differently and be full of light, hope, peace, and confidence.

Pattern of Transformation: Wholeness

As we recognize and change our old beliefs by listening to the Lord and taking in his Word, so our thoughts and emotional lives change. The old pattern of thinking begins to break apart and it reduces in intensity and frequency. New patterns form a new framework for our emotional lives. Our characters are changed as Christ is formed in us. We develop wholeness and maturity, taking responsibility for our choices. We give up our investment in the misbeliefs and take in the truth. We see this process sketched out in Romans 12:2 where Paul exhorts, "Let your minds be remade and your whole nature thus transformed" (NEB).

The diagram that follows show graphically how the transformation process works.

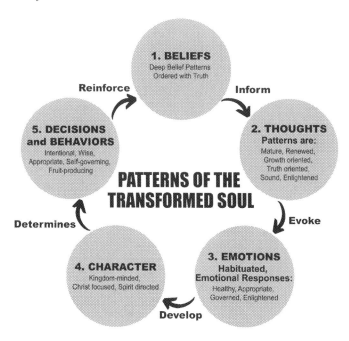

Practical Way to Change our Thoughts

To change our thought patterns, our wills must be engaged. This is not about striving. It's not a teeth-clenching, "I-can-do-this-on-my-own" struggle, but a collaboration with the Lord. We say yes with our whole being and align with him. We choose to battle our distorted thoughts, irrational ways of responding, and darkened feelings, knowing the Lord supplies the empowering grace.

Since our personal approach is vital, I'd like to demonstrate changing our thoughts with a simple acronym: ARC. ARC stands for *arrest, renew,* and *cultivate.* Dark, unhealthy thoughts and emotions are stirred and aided by the kingdom of darkness and often become part of our default, but with the assistance of the Holy Spirit we can become aware of them. We then engage our wills to step toward the Lord, empowered by his Spirit, **arresting** the thought and interrupting the flow. For example, when I was stuck in a loop of negative thinking, the Lord whispered to me: *Flip the switch.* This became my signal to stop, to arrest that thought flow, and to turn my mind to good things. This works for me because every time I think of that prompt, I visualize a railroad switch that enables a train to be redirected onto another track. When I become aware of my negative or introspective thinking, I stop and flip the switch onto another track.

Arresting the sequence of dark thoughts is only the beginning. Next, we keep moving toward the Lord, to the true and good, by **renewing** our minds. That's the new track we run on. We replace our old thoughts with new ones based in truth. Because thoughts travel in neural pathways, by meditating on the Word and choosing it over and over, we create new neural pathways in the brain and develop a redeemed belief system that is based in Spirit and truth. Our hearts get formed as we take in the Word, especially during difficult times. It's something we can choose—where we set our attention and what we take in. We keep adopting the new, receiving it deeply into our hearts by the power of the Holy Spirit, **cultivating** it.

To cultivate means to incorporate God's truth and ways into our lives, to deeply root them by practicing the truth choice by choice and thought by thought. This enables us to become anchored, steadfast, encouraged, and established. As we stay nourished in the Lord, we are strengthened to continue being transformed. This means establishing daily habits for dwelling on God's Word and listening to him as we pray over our concerns.

As our new, healthier thoughts become established through discipline and cultivation, more is possible. New frameworks begin to be built, working against our normal default thinking. We need to stop believing everything we think, let go of diseased thinking, and build the new and good. Then even more is possible.

Journaling Exercise with Arrest, Renew, Cultivate

God's truth will illumine, sustain, and anchor us. As we take it in and meditate on it, exchanging our old beliefs for his truth, we are powerfully renewed, redirected, and changed. His life begins to permeate us; his Spirit creates new understanding.

God's exchange program takes the words from old wounds, and from the world, the flesh, and the devil—words that are crippling and menacing—and arrests them and exchanges them for life-giving truth! Write out these words and release them to the cross, asking God to take them. Then, listen and receive what he is giving you in exchange, renewing your mind. By doing this, you are replacing the toxic with the true, the broken with the whole. God's Word unfailingly bears fruit in due season, restoring us to wholeness.

These are helpful steps:

1. Begin by being still, acknowledging his presence, and thanking him that he is with you. (This is practicing his presence.)
2. Honestly write out the negative, shaming thoughts you have been having.
3. Take time to listen to what God is saying now to *arrest* and replace the lies and to *renew* your mind.
4. When he gives a scripture or a word of truth and encouragement, record it, and respond with thanks and worship.
5. Continue to meditate on and *cultivate* what God has given.

Prayer

Lord, thank you for giving me a wonderful mind, an intellect, the ability to think well, to remember, and to analyze.

Forgive my passivity in seeking your transformation of my thought life. Forgive me for allowing old ways to remain and govern my thinking. Forgive me for letting old wounds and old experiences tell me false things about who I am, who you are, and how life is to be. Forgive me for letting the poison take effect. I particularly repent of believing _____ (fill in the blank).

I expose these things to your beautiful light and banish them from my life, from the least lie to the deepest pattern. Lord, break generational iniquity in the ways I learned to think and in the things I think about, whether biases or prejudices—any way of seeing the world apart from your truth. The things of which I am not aware, I ask you to enlighten and to bring awareness. I need your empowering grace to renew my mind according to the truth and to form healthy habits of thought. Thank you, Holy Spirit, that you give me that empowering grace.

I not only want to think well and sanely, but I also want to love and trust you with my mind. Give me the very mind of Christ. You have given me power, love, and a sound mind. You have given me the ability to think well, with freedom and fullness of peace and joy. I receive your mind, your thoughts. I thank you that I can think spiritual thoughts because I have your Word and your Spirit within.

Lord, break me free from the torment of compulsions and chaos in my thought life. Thank you for the power of the cross to accomplish this. I repent of letting my mind dominate other parts of my soul. Where I have separated my rational mind from the other parts of my soul, Lord, I repent. I welcome you in and ask you to connect, restore, and order each part within my soul, formed together.

For Introspection:

Lord, I recognize I've been practicing this self-centered, dark habit. I ask you to strengthen me to decide, repent, and walk anew. Grant me your grace just now.

Father, I repent of trusting my own resources and devices to manage life, and of the unbelief that accompanies that. I repent of the wrong kind of self-love, where I have set up myself as my own idol-god. I dethrone that idol-god now in the name of Jesus.

I repent of the practice and of the stronghold I have developed as a way of managing life, apart from your truth and ways. I receive your forgiveness now.

I choose now not to dwell on the past or to project into the future. I am deciding that I will live present, and if suppressed anxiety and pain come up, I will seek you, rather than covering them. I choose to live present with you, experiencing all of life. Where I need to battle to gain back the ground, strengthen and equip me, Lord.

Where demonic torment has entered from the long practice of introspection, I now bind it and send it to the cross. Lord, heal my mind and anoint me with the mind of Christ. I pray for peace to come now, for quiet and ease to enter my mind as your love floods me. Teach me how to think well with a renewed mind; teach me how to think with your thoughts and to abide in your presence.

Daily help me know what small steps to take so that I can become anchored in the good and the new. Lead me in your truth as you have promised. I step now toward great hope as you heal my mind and thoughts.

Recap

In our spiritual formation God begins to heal our ways of knowing, and especially the deep patterns of our thought processes. We begin to realize the importance of our thought lives and recognize our vital responsibility to have renewed minds in Christ. As we deal with strongholds in our thinking, with our wills we can learn to set our minds on thoughts of wholeness and holiness. Now let's turn our attention to another way of knowing, that of the receptive mind.

4

THE RECEPTIVE MIND

When the Lord begins working in us, he recreates every capacity of our souls, preparing every part of our inner lives to be filled with his Spirit. Often, the first things he deals with are our capacities for knowledge through both the rational and receptive minds, because the more we can perceive, recognize, and understand rightly, the more we are able to know and cooperate with him.

The receptive mind includes the heart instruments of intuition and imagination. This mind "enters into" by perceiving, sensing, receiving impressions and intuitions, and taking in revelation. It has to do with how we know God and how we know others—how we connect.[38] We have this capacity because we have first been loved and created by him, and in response we learn to be receptive.

Christopher West wrote, "Every human being's first posture as a creature is one of *receptivity* to the gift of God. Indeed, it is impossible for a creature to give anything if he has not first received."[39] Referring to this idea, Eugene Peterson, translator of *The Message* Bible, indicated that when ideas for the text came to him, they came when he was in a state of receptivity.[40] He was collaborating with the Holy Spirit in his writing.

The rational mind uses logic and analysis to measure and understand. With our intellects, we can put into words and execute what we have

---

[38] Carla Waterman, "Capacities and Motions of the Soul."
[39] Christopher West, *Theology of the Body Explained* (Boston, MA: Pauline Books & Media, 2003), 108.
[40] Winn Collier, *A Burning in My Bones* (Colorado Springs, CO: Waterbrook Press, 2021), 263.

entered into and known with our receptive minds. The two minds are created to operate in tandem, but often we have one mind overactive and one dormant. We can be overly rational and unable to be connected, or very connected and unable to be rational. We often need healing to connect the two minds for fullness in our souls.

We understand in diverse ways with these two minds because they have different capacities. One is entering in, and one is understanding what we have entered into. Today, culturally, we have increasing analysis without having experienced and entered into what we are talking about.

For example, I went to Rome, "Bella Roma," a few years ago. In preparation, I read about the city and the Vatican and looked at pictures to familiarize myself with what I would encounter. But reading a travel guide, seeing photographs with comments of others' experiences, is not the same as being in a country with its people, industry, smells, landscape, shops, cuisine, and art. A travel guide is a way in, and helped me prepare for what was to come, but I didn't really "know" until I was there to experience the city. Once in Rome, I sat on a bench in the Sistine Chapel looking at the ceiling frescoes and inviting the presence of the Lord. A priest asked for holy silence, spoke briefly, and prayed beautifully. I sat in awe, sensing and receiving the Lord's presence! This was quite different from looking with interest at travel guides and photographs. I had entered in.

So it is with many Christians. We read the guidebook, know so much about the Christian journey, and see where we are supposed to go, but never actually go there because we lack the capacity to enter in. Our two minds aren't both engaged. Only the rational is, and so that is the only reality we live in—the only way we know how to know. We extract truths from scripture without entering in, and we are much poorer for it. This is knowing apart from faith, apart from fully engaging our hearts.

Interceding for the Ephesian believers, Paul wrote: "I pray that the eyes of your heart may be enlightened in order that you may know the hope to which he has called you, the riches of his glorious inheritance in his holy people, and his incomparably great power for us who believe" (Eph 1:18–19 NIV). One thing we need to do is ask the Lord to open the eyes of our hearts. He really wants to do this for us. Jesus said, "But blessed are your eyes because they see, and your ears because they hear" (Mt 13:16 NIV).

Receptivity is our inheritance, and we need to ask for our inheritance to be given to us. For instance, one Easter morning I was meditating on the triumphal entry of Jesus into Jerusalem on the donkey, and I could see and feel myself as one of the palm-waving crowd. I entered into that scripture: with the eyes of my heart, I saw Jesus look at me, really look at me, as he passed by. It was a beautiful, life-filled encounter. I felt deeply seen, known, and loved. I had an imaginative experience as my receptive mind took in what the Lord was imparting to me.

Pause and Reflect

Stop and ask the Lord to open the eyes of your heart in a new way, to experience more of his presence through receptivity. If you have any uncertainty about asking the Lord to help you experience more of his presence in this way, bring that to him as well.

Receptivity

Have you ever felt as if you were communicating with someone who is "not there"? I've had many experiences with people that felt like mere transactions. When an individual is unable to be present and truly vulnerable, both giving and receiving, a relationship cannot progress. We have to be present and receptive for walls to go down and to reach outside of ourselves to others. Receptivity involves the opening of our souls. We have to be willing to be changed by our encounters—even by the pain of others.

The receptivity of "entering in" needs to happen with other people, with nature and beauty, and in our relationship with the Lord. As we let down our defenses, we become willing to be changed by him. We often have places inside where we want God to go only so far and no further. We put up a wall of self-centeredness and may not even know in what particular area the problem is. There is some reluctance or resistance, perhaps based in a fear or a misperception of God—something that needs to be changed.

We can always pray: "Lord, show me what barrier keeps me from being in your presence and listening to you—what keeps me apart from you." Or we may have receptivity for a while and then suddenly come to a wall. It's never his reluctance to engage us; we are the one who put up barriers. When we acknowledge those walls and that we don't want them, we do our part to break the self-centeredness and invite the Lord in. He will put his finger on the problem soon enough.[41]

Two Instruments of Receptivity

Jonathan Edwards wrote that God can't be known by intellect alone but must be loved "through … a participatory way of knowing," which is the "feeling mind." He called this "a sense of the heart."[42] This feeling mind can also be called the receptive heart, which has two specific instruments that operate together: intuition and imagination. We must reclaim both of these instruments in our souls.

The voice of intuition is *I sense; I know by sensing.* The voice of imagination is *I see and envision; I know by seeing.*

Intuition—Intuition is a capacity we are born with, to know by sensing and taking in. This is an ability to enter in and pick up emotional knowledge of someone else at a profound level. For instance, babies know when they are safe or not, and whether their caretaker is tense with them or nurturing. Little ones can't think rationally yet, but they do intuit. Intuition brings knowledge by connection. When a baby takes in the being—the knowledge—of another, this knowing transcends reason.

Intuition is also developed by life experience. We are born with the capacity for intuition, and we also develop it because we have been engaged in many life situations. We often know things without being able to explain what we specifically know. (I found this was true in many years of counseling practice.) This often comes from the things we have done so often. They finally come naturally because we enter in by a whole different way. For instance, there is a difference in a child performing in a recital

[41] Waterman, "Capacities and Motions of the Soul."
[42] Belden C. Lane, "Jonathan Edwards on Beauty, Desire and the Sensory World," *Theological Studies* 65, no. 1 (2004): 58.

and the worship leader who knows how to enter in. The negative side to this way of knowing is that we can walk into a situation, such as family, and intuit something is really wrong. Then we may react strongly because we have mentally stored experiences of similar situations in the past that were unsafe or unstable. The pattern of association triggers reactions to similar dynamics.

Intuition is also a spiritual capacity that enables us to see and understand. To know the Lord and all the good and true things in life, we must have our hearts opened to receive. This capacity must be awakened in us by the Holy Spirit, and all the gifts of the Spirit come through the receptive mind.

Our culture frequently defines intuition as an immature kind of knowledge, and rationality as mature and logical. As such, intuition is devalued. But intuition is a true way of knowing, not a secondary, inferior way. It is not flighty and not to be discounted as it often is.

Because intuition is relational knowledge, it can't be acquired without entering in. This means that we have to connect and pay attention to the relationship. There is no other way to learn than to really be present. This is so necessary for our relationships with those close to us, and also with God as we practice his presence. We can intuit the presence of the Lord around us in worship; we can intuit the ministry of angels in our midst. Our heart senses these things. The heart's deep way of knowing takes us into these realities.

God always wants to deposit fresh things within us. He's given us a receptive mind—the heart—to take in these things of the Spirit. Hebrews 5:14 tells us that the mature have their *senses* trained to discern by long practice. When we are alive and connected to God, we are maturing in our receptive minds, in the intuitive and imaginative faculties, in our ability to receive and know that what we are receiving is from him. We train our senses because we are alive in Christ. This spiritual intuition can be developed as we keep our hearts open, asking God to give us discernment and the ability to "pick up" the things of the Spirit and how and where he is moving. Wonderfully, we can learn this by practice.

Pause and Reflect

How have you thought of intuition? Have you devalued it or recognized it as a key to walking in faith and light, truth and righteousness? If you have devalued it, ask God to forgive you now and to restore your intuitive faculty.

Imagination—Besides intuition, we have imagination, which is the image-making faculty created by God to make symbols. We are created to symbolize. Our hearts take in and "think" in symbols. Symbols bring thought, feeling, and intuition together to bind truths to our souls. Jesus taught in stories and parables, often from everyday life and agriculture, because he was bringing truth through story and symbol. Symbols and pictures are the language the heart speaks and are much richer and more mysterious than intellectual reasoning alone. When we think of Father God, we already have a symbol in our hearts of a father. It's why we often need to have our hearts healed and re-symbolized with new truth and meaning. As we seek the Lord and seek his Word, we will find that our heart symbols are being transformed into the good, true, and holy.

The Lord places symbols in our hearts so we can access them in our minds. These are vehicles for the heart to communicate with the mind because symbols have meaning to us. We want to respond to the Lord, to the things he's depositing in our hearts, so they can come into our rational minds, and we can activate what he's giving. (An example of this might be a dream from the Lord.)

Christians tend to fear the imagination and may even stigmatize it as evil. But imagination is not evil in itself. Our imaginations are not to be the devil's playground; they are meant to be the workshop of the Holy Spirit, of heaven! Imagination has been called the womb of faith because what you can imagine, what you can see in your heart, you can have faith for. Imagination lights up our faith. When we read the first chapter of Ephesians we grow in awe of the deep, high, vast, staggering largeness of God's world and kingdom. Paul really stretches our imaginations here as we consider this incredible love and the beauty of the movement of the Holy Spirit.

A truly imaginative experience is an intuition of the real. It's not the ability to have a vivid imagination, or to fantasize. As an example of this, years ago I was designing a house for my family on some acreage, praying over the creation of it, and suddenly "saw" a cottage beside it that blended with the design of our home. Although I hadn't considered it before, I realized it would be for my father, who was elderly and in a wheelchair at that time. I didn't even know if he'd want to live on our property, as that had never been discussed. When I first presented the possibility, he discounted the idea. But as I left it before the Lord, believing what I had seen in my imagination was from him, my father changed his mind, and the cottage was built alongside my home. I had seen the reality of what God was intending. As a result, my father was surrounded by family and cared for there until a few months before his death.

"To receive a word or picture from God is to know the true imagination in operation. The truly imaginative experience is an intuition of the real."[43] When I saw the cottage, I had an intuition of the real. By faith, I received it from the Lord, and waited for him to bring it about. (I also got busy with the design.) Imaginative knowledge helps us perceive and enter into the unseen. Though it may be unseen, it is reality. We sometimes think of imagination as seeing what is unreal, but it's really about what is unseen yet very real.

Imagination consists of story, picture, and symbol. For this reason, we must have a deep respect for the power of symbol in children's hearts and what they take in as truth. We need to give them symbols with honor and meaning so they can rise to them. This is why we should read good books to them, have good conversations with them, tell them our stories, and explain thoughts, ideas, and concepts using symbols they can take in.

When we open our hearts to receive from the Lord, as well as from others and from nature, we receive that good into our imaginations. We are acknowledging the real in an unseen dimension. This is a large component of faith because "faith is pre-eminently the receptive faculty."[44]

Since imagination is an image-making faculty, it goes beyond the cognitive. Just read Lewis's *Chronicles of Narnia* for great examples in symbol that draw us to greater realities. Consider Aslan, the faithful, untamed, tender lion who sang Narnia into being then sacrificed himself;

[43] Leanne Payne, *Listening Prayer* (Grand Rapids, MI: Hamewith Books, a division of Baker Publishing Group, 1994), 159.
[44] Meyer, *The Secret of Guidance*, 33.

Reepicheep, the fierce pilgrim mouse who pursued his destiny despite great difficulty; Puddleglum, the pessimist who resisted enchantments and seductive lies; and Prince Caspian, who yearned for the real Narnia and learned to be a warrior. These wonderful characters serve as symbols that speak deeply to our hearts.

We are creatures who symbolize. And if the symbols we hold in our hearts are distorted, we will be distorted in our responses to life. Why? Because symbols shape our reality. For instance, where we have a symbol of father that is not the true, tender, and strong masculine, we will have distorted ideas about God the Father.

Reality is so much bigger than the limitations of our words, so we need symbols, ritual, ceremony, metaphor, pictures, narrative, gestures, dreams, and visions to fill out reality. Jesus spoke in parables and pictures rich in symbol. The mystery of God is great, and God helps us by giving symbols that communicate to us. God as Father is an incredible symbol. Or Jesus as lion, lamb, good shepherd, or the one with fire in his eyes. We have Christian symbols: cross, altar, bread, wine, water, dove, oil, and other material things that speak to our senses of his presence. The Holy Spirit brings life to all of these.

There are so many symbols in scripture, including real people. In Genesis 32, Jacob, a liar and supplanter, encounters the Lord. He wrestles with God all night and leaves with a physical limp, but Jacob is changed forever. What hope a symbol like that brings to our hearts.

Scripture is full of stories and metaphors to give symbols to our hearts. Another example is when Elisha prayed that his servant's eyes would be opened to see "the hills full of horses and chariots of fire all around" (2 Kgs 6:15–18 NIV). Once our eyes are opened to "see" like the servant, our holy imaginations are lit up with faith. Can you just imagine seeing what that servant saw? That was the reality of God!

However, other scriptural stories illustrate how metaphorical images can stir fear and stifle holy imagination.

In Numbers 13, ten of Moses's dozen spies, upon returning from their exploration of Canaan, brought a pessimistic report: "The land is full of giants, and we are like grasshoppers." This painted a frightful picture in the imaginations of their fellow Israelites and brought a stop to their journey for many years.

But the other two spies, Joshua and Caleb, confidently shared a contradictory, hopeful report and painted a picture of a beautiful and abundant land, a land where the giants would be "prey" and not predator (Nm 14:9). This picture of abundance and overcoming painted by Joshua and Caleb deposited a different image in the imaginations of the Israelites—one of God's promises. But it would be many years before God's people would be able to enter into that.

The more we are able to engage our vital imaginations—as Joshua and Caleb did—the more abundantly the power of the Spirit works within us. Ephesians 3:20 says, "Now to him who is able to do immeasurably more than all we ask or imagine, according to his power that is at work within us" (NIV). We need to ask the Lord to help us engage in asking, imagining, and seeing his power at work within us.

God created matter, so he is able to bless and hallow what he's created and use it for his purposes. For example, baptism in water, anointing with oil, communion with bread and wine. In these, we are touching what is divine in the human, material way. When we take communion, we enter in—our receptive mind receives and takes in. When we sing psalms and hymns, the symbols we take in are healing and stirring.

Water is profoundly symbolic as well. Consider the flood, the parting of the Red Sea, the water gushing from the rock, baptism, the river of life in the book of Revelation, and so many other examples. God paints glorious pictures in scripture not simply for us to analyze, but also so that we can enter into them. We can go to the throne and see the living water mentioned in Ezekiel and in Revelation. We can know that the Lord's water washes us for, "Though your sins are as scarlet, they shall become as white as snow" (Is 1:18 NASB). Water is a rich symbol behind which is the reality of his living, moving presence.

What are some symbols of scripture that speak to you? A favorite of mine is the "oaks of righteousness" in Isaiah 61:3. There is a rich promise of how God's Spirit will come and move over his people to bind up their wounds, comfort them, and set them free. Then, "They will be called oaks of righteousness, a planting of the LORD for the display of his splendor" (NIV). Ancient ruins will be rebuilt, devastations restored and renewed. Quite a symbol, this magnificent oak tree. My study windows look out on oaks, and they fill me with the life of green renewal and hope. I am able to have true receptivity with those magnificent trees; I take them in! And I know he has promised that I am becoming like one of these. Even in the dead of winter I am reminded that all of this takes time—season after season of growth and maturity. What looks barren is only bare now; there is real life in the depth of that tree that will bring it again to leafing. I can participate in that reality.

Mystery and Gift

Some mysteries of God are so great that we can't understand them; and yet we do participate in them. Who can read Isaiah 6 and not envision the Lord on a high throne, his train filling the temple, seraphim flying around crying "holy," the door posts shaking, and the room filled with smoke? No wonder Isaiah was undone. When we begin to recognize that we are seeing the real, and when we start to realize what our imaginations are created for, we begin to experience life. It inspires us with mystery and awe. At the highest level, imagination is the ability to see, hear, and receive from God the true and real. But if our imaginations are dull or darkened, we lose our sense of wonder, beauty, and curiosity.

C. S. Lewis and Oswald Chambers both wrote that imagination is the greatest gift we have. When Lewis was a young man and a "rational atheist," he read a fantasy novel by the Christian writer George MacDonald. Lewis said that it baptized his imagination. It changed his mind, awakening a yearning for something else, which he later called holiness. This is the great power of imagination. Alexander Whyte, in his old book *Lord, Teach Us to Pray*, said that imagination is a gift of God's goodness to us. It is both the "noblest intellectual attribute" and something "even more to every spiritually minded man."[45]

To be truly imaginative does not mean we have a train of images coursing through the brain. It is not just coming up with some picture or idea; it is the intuition of the real emerging as thought or image. For instance, in Rome I stood transfixed in St. Peter's Basilica looking at Michelangelo's *Pieta,* the pathos and beauty of all it represented. Later, I

---

[45] Alexander Whyte, *Lord, Teach Us to Pray* (Yuma, CO: Jawbone Digital, 2012), 145.

knew I was taking in the true masculine when I stood before a replica of Michelangelo's *David*.

The point of setting our imaginations before God is not to make up our own images but to receive what God gives. During my devotional time, I sometimes like to pull up a chair for the Father and invite him to sit with me for a few minutes. Other times, I use my imagination to bathe in his love, swim in his river, and stand at the cross and offer Jesus my heart. This is the real and the true of what is unseen with my eyes but seen by my heart.

Pause and Reflect

Let's deliberately set ourselves before God just now by sitting with him and asking a question. Ask the Lord how he sees you in a symbolic picture. Invite him to give you a picture from his heart. Write it out in your spiritual journal and ask him about what he is showing you.

When I did this once, I saw a sunflower. As I researched that, I found how rich it was in symbolism and was able to rejoice that this is what the Lord saw in me.

Sin Taints the Receptive Heart

If we want to have the eyes of our hearts fully opened, we can't be voluntarily taking in profane symbols and then expect the Lord to use them in our hearts to create beautiful unseen realities. We are daily assaulted by symbols from our culture that we don't need to take in. Of course, it's not just about the absence of profane symbols in our imaginations, but about what symbols we should and do feed our imaginations every day.

Many have recognized the power of the imagination and have misused it for their own ends. We must train our imaginations like we train our wills. We must engage our wills to picture what is good, true, and beautiful, not what we dread and fear. We have control over the images on the screen of our own imaginations. Where we set our imaginations is so important. As Alicia Britt Chole writes, "this is not about the shutting down of our imaginations but the disciplining of them" so we don't invest in "untruth." "Disciplining our imaginations can be an enormous challenge, especially when we perceive ourselves as deprived of affirmation, attention, or acceptance."[46]

Denying the use of imagination and shutting it off creates depleted lives. But misusing our imaginations also creates impoverishment as we live so far below what God designed us for. Any time we have filled our hearts with images of evil, perversity, sensuality, and inferiority, this diminishes our beautiful imaginative capacities. Our imaginations need to be cleansed of things we've watched, heard, seen, and experienced that have deposited their images within. As Frank Lake wrote, "We must change. We take our eyes off our libidinal picture gallery and fix them, wide open, on Christ. Our minds need prizing [prying] open to new truth and a double insight—into our misery and Christ's majesty."[47]

As we pray for cleansing of what we have taken in, we sanctify again the imagination through the blood of Christ. Even when we have a bad dream, we can pull the images out of our imaginations and offer them to Jesus on the cross.

Our imagination is so wonderful that we don't want to cloud and compromise it with things that hinder us from receiving the things of the Spirit. We don't have to shamefully stuff down vile or distorted images that emerge as the Lord is dealing with us. The Lord desires to uncover impurities so that we might bring them to the cross for cleansing and healing. Then, with cleansed and Spirit-filled imaginations, united with our intellects, we can create and step into what he inspires.

Prayer

For cleansing the imagination—Lord, grant me the grace to confess my sins and any profane images I've taken in. Grant me the grace to forgive others whose sins have caused an imprint on my soul. I name them now.

Forgive me also for misusing my imagination by fantasizing about the things I should not.

[46] Alicia Britt Chole, *Anonymous* (Nashville, TN: W Publishing Group, 2006), 121.

[47] Frank Lake, *Clinical Theology, Abridged* 1987, 71.

I ask you to bring anything to my mind that has settled into my imagination—anything false or profane or dangerous or damaging. I pull that right up and out of my mind and send it to the cross. With the eyes of my heart, I want to see what you are doing with those images, whether they are pornographic, frightful, demonic, a diseased fantasy, violent, occultic, or traumatic. (Take your time with this.)

Lord, I name these things so that I might have authority over them and not stay in shame. Take each image into yourself on the cross and set me free. Cleanse my imagination of these things. For this you died that I might be free. I fully receive your cleansing.

Now, Lord, fill and replace the void where images were released. By your Holy Spirit replace the old images with good ones. Stir up long dormant gifts and bring new life to my imagination. Anoint my imagination for holy things.

To open the receptive mind—Holy Spirit, stir in my heart. May I know I am secure, and that I can open my heart with vulnerability because of your love. Lord, forgive me where I've chosen to stay in the safety of my own overly rational mind. Forgive me where I've valued my intellect over my heart. In the same way, where I've stayed too much in the intuitive and haven't seen the good of the rational, forgive me also. You created me wonderfully so that both minds can be integrated. I now receive your forgiveness.

Please strengthen and connect both my rational and my intuitive mind. Lord, unite my intellect, intuition, and imagination; heal the divide between my head and heart. Show me any walls in my soul that keep me from receiving from you, from seeing and listening to you. I don't want anything between us.

Awaken and reorient my intuitive heart. Open the eyes of my heart. Awaken my soul in every capacity. Create new things within my receptive mind, Lord.

Homework

Practice sitting quietly with the Lord, inviting him to sit there with you. By faith, open your receptive mind to see or hear anything his Spirit is bringing to you.

Recap

The receptive mind, both intuition and imagination, is about connection. It perceives and knows in a different way from the rational mind, but both are necessary for fully knowing and understanding. The receptive mind enters into and takes in what the rational mind can then put into words and execute. We need intuition and imagination fully alive and open to the Holy Spirit, and we can practice developing this.

Next let's look at how the conscience functions in our souls.

5

THE CONSCIENCE

The Guardian

The conscience guards the gates into our souls. The voice of the conscience is *I guard, or I watch.* As gatekeeper a good conscience keeps in righteous and worthy thoughts and choices while barring the unrighteous and unworthy from entry. If wrong conduct has occurred, the function of the conscience is to produce true guilt so that wrong can be faced and remedied. Hebrews 13:18 says, "We are sure that we have a good conscience, desiring to conduct ourselves honorably in all things" (NASB). This describes the function of a healthy conscience; it is motivated toward honor and good behavior.

We are all born with a conscience, an inborn sense of "knowing" right and wrong. The conscience is an inner instinct, but unaided by the Holy Spirit it can cause us to feel conflicted, pulling us between self-accusation and defensiveness. As with every part of our souls, we need strength of will and the influence of the Spirit of truth to set this antagonism right. We are born with a conscience, but we still have to develop a healthy one. The Lord will impart his life into that development.

We need to know how to protect and nurture our conscience because we are daily assaulted with the unholy. Developing a conscience as the gatekeeper is essential for the protection of the righteous life within us; not to protect our own conscience invites compromise. Our conscience helps us know and apply appropriate moral principles to specific actions. It is the gateway where our souls are presented with moral choices, distinguishing right from wrong, able to feel true conviction and true guilt. The Holy Spirit works in and through a healthy conscience.

A conscience freed, ordered, and filled with the Holy Spirit will go far in keeping us full of integrity. Our conscience needs to be trained by wise habits. Then it can warn us when something is wrong and point us toward wisdom and the good. What the conscience awakens us to, wisdom can direct us through. When we are faced with decisions, godly wisdom understands the complexity and nuances of a situation.[48]

Paul said that he wanted to have a good, clear conscience: "I strive always to keep my conscience clear before God and man" (Acts 24:16 NIV). That took the moral effort of an engaged will. In his second letter to the Corinthians Paul said, "The testimony of our conscience, that in holiness and godly sincerity, not in fleshly wisdom but in the grace of God, we have conducted ourselves in the world, and especially toward you" (2 Cor 1:12 NASB). Our conscience testifies to behaviors and attitudes, and Paul was indicating that his conscience testified that he was walking in holiness, sincerity, wisdom, and grace.

Peter instructed those in his care this way: "Be on your guard lest … you fall from your own steadfastness" (2 Pt 3:17 NASB). The conscience is the first guard at the door to warn us of wrong influences. Since we can be influenced by others and yield to their persuasions, we want our conscience to be activated, strong, and clear. We want to be able to recognize and resist such wrong persuasions.

We are not to be judged by another's conscience (1 Cor 10:29) and neither are we to wound the weak conscience of another (1 Cor 8:12). We can offer our opinions and present our convictions, but we don't trespass the conscience of others by telling them what they should do or ought to believe, particularly in gray areas. That only puts people on the defensive. Then they will resist the thing we most want to persuade them of.

---

[48] Waterman, "Capacities and Motions of the Soul."

Clear Conscience

A clear conscience is not burdened with guilt and self-accusation. It is at ease, free from undue scruples, at peace within. How do we get this clear, peace-filled conscience? Our Father provides us with a grace-filled antidote to guilt: repentance of real sin, not just guilty feelings. Unease of conscience is constructive when it causes us to pause and examine a course of action or to realize where we have done wrong. For example, David cut off the edge of Saul's robe in a cave and afterward his conscience bothered him (literally, "his heart struck him") for dishonoring the king (1 Sm 24:5 NASB). This is different from self-condemnation (which issues a verdict on the whole self) because it is a clear and specific conviction and points to a need for repentance and a remedy.

When we are disquieted and examine our conscience, we should not practice introspection, where we gaze at ourselves and center on ourselves. The best way to enlighten our conscience and discern our real sins is to look to God, to reflect on his Word as our mirror and let it instruct us (Jas 1:23–24).

The Spirit also instructs our conscience. During the 1970s I was in graduate school and was given a stipend as a teaching assistant. I needed a book for the upcoming course I was to teach. The department had ordered one, but the deadline was looming to prepare my syllabus and I wanted the book immediately. Reasoning that I could pop over to the university bookstore, slip the book into my briefcase, and then replace it when the new book came in, I hatched my plan. (I know!) Those were the days before electronic scanners and alarms were in use, so I thought my scheme would work. I remember exactly where I was. As I walked up the stairs to the fourth-floor office I shared with other young graduate assistants, a verse came into my consciousness, emerging from the inside and floating up into my awareness: "... providing for honest things, not only in the sight of the Lord, but also in the sight of men" (2 Cor 8:21 KJV). Immediate conviction; immediate change of plans. I never took the book.

By staying in the Word often, I had given the Holy Spirit a library to choose from and choose he did. Martin Luther said this so well: "My conscience is captive to the Word of God." The Word instructed my conscience, giving me a choice that helped me be honest and keep a clear conscience. By carnal reasoning I had almost abdicated to sin, but my conscience warned me, and with my will I closed the gate to the enemy. In Christ, we can live with an unviolated conscience.

Pause and Reflect

What have you been taught about your conscience? Have you thought about your conscience as a significant capacity of your soul? In what ways can you see that it is necessary and helpful?

Have you ever asked the Lord to help you walk in the integrity of a clear conscience? Would you pause and do that now? The Holy Spirit will be responsive to this prayer.

Are you feeling any unease of conscience just now? It can be helpful to sit with the Lord and ask him, "Is the unease I am feeling true guilt?" If not, what do you need to release?

The Over-Functioning Conscience

The conscience ought to keep intruders out and good things in. When it is functioning well, we know what to keep out. And it is much easier to stop the battle at the gate (Is 28:6). For example, when we feel the first stirrings of jealousy, bitterness, or lust, we can quickly decide not to allow them entry. But if the conscience is not functioning well, we have little ability to keep out intruders and to live in freedom.

If something has gone awry in the activation of our conscience during childhood, it may be overly alert at the gate. In that case, peace in the ability to make wise choices is difficult to find. An oversensitive and overscrupulous conscience makes us too cautious, easily shamed, introspective, and uncertain—real bondage indeed. It is as if we have closed our gates too tightly, too heavily guarding the city by our own internal laws. This is not the freedom of the Spirit but a false voice of the malformed conscience. We may even interpret scriptures in a legalistic way to keep our conscience quiet so that we can feel righteous. In this way, our legalism exchanges strict obedience to our own moral standards for a living faith.

The voice of the conscience is part of the whole symphony of our souls. But when the conscience stands alone, without interdependence on other faculties of our souls, we are led to extremes. Many religious groups are based on inflated convictions of conscience, and we sometimes find in the church a similar overscrupulousness.

Individually, we may feel a constant and often vague sense that somehow we have fallen short. It is really a posture of staying vigilant, so we won't get punished, perhaps an echo of childhood, and is based on "irrational or … inauthentic" standards within.[49] An overscrupulous conscience creates internal accusation, shame, unease, and self-doubt— false guilt trapped in a hyperactive conscience.

If there is guilt, it needs to be real guilt that points us to repentance. We may keep working to free ourselves and feel better, but because of our own inner legalism, we can't. That legalism gets mixed with our perceptions of God, and to be freed we need a true vision of who he really is: our complete redeemer, our holiness, our righteousness. The Holy Spirit wants to operate within our true, healed conscience to bring clean conviction and to inform our actions. Then we can rest and have confidence in the Lord. He alone pardons sin, forgives iniquity, imparts righteousness, and allows us to walk in real peace. (See Micah 7:18–20). He isn't waiting to punish us; he is waiting to free us.

The enemy can take our desire to do good and trouble us with it, making us painstakingly careful. We have to learn to ignore these scruples and trust ourselves to the one who brings peace to our conscience. We should resolve what we can and move on instead of striving and introspecting over our choices. We can live without undue regret, striving, tension, and scrupulosity concerning the past because our past is covered by his blood.

---

[49] Leanne Payne, *Restoring the Christian Soul Through Healing Prayer* (Wheaton, Il: Crossway Books a division of Good News Publishers, 1991), 148.

The Under-Functioning Conscience

While some have an over-functioning conscience, others have dulled their conscience, forming one that is under-functioning. The guard at the gate is not alert. We pollute and sear our conscience by sinning. We weaken and dull it by defilement or ignorance. Roy Hession succinctly wrote: "Many of us have neglected the referee's whistle so often and for so long that we have ceased to hear it."[50]

We have freedom in Christ, but if we use our freedom wrongly, our conscience will shut down from repeated violation. This creates a false voice that assures us all is well. The extreme of an under-functioning conscience is a sociopath or psychopath who has no conscience because it has ceased to function and warn. Karl Menninger wrote: "The human conscience is like the police: it may be eluded, stifled, drugged, or bribed. But not without cost."[51]

Our consciences become darkened as we ignore the light over time. In areas where we have sinned repeatedly, we become defiled and dull. We see this described several places in the scriptures. In 2 Chronicles 29:34, the priests dulled their conscience in regard to preparing and sanctifying themselves to serve. Passover had stopped because of their disobedience and had to be reactivated under King Hezekiah. In Malachi 2:16, God warned the men who were divorcing their wives: "Pay attention to your conscience, and do not be unfaithful" (NET). They had overridden their consciences and deceitfully divorced their wives, putting them away instead of choosing to love and care for them. In Jeremiah 6:15, the prophets and priests did not feel shame; they did not "even know how to blush" (NIV). When our consciences are derailed like this, our emotional and moral being is also disordered. We can do all sorts of things we ought not when the conscience is weak.

John 3:19 also offers a picture of fallen conscience: "The light has come into the world, and people loved the darkness rather than the light because their works were evil" (ESV). We tend to shrink from the light

---

[50] Roy Hession, *The Calvary Road* (Fort Washington, PA: Christian Literature Crusade, 1950), 33.
[51] Karl Menninger, *Whatever Became of Sin?* (New York, NY: Hawthorn Books, 1973), 198.

when we have sinned. We want to hide in shame. But if we step into the light, we receive cleansing. By grace, we are given a way to walk so that our consciences work well. We see this in Acts 2:37–38 when Peter was preaching at Pentecost. Those listening were "pierced to the heart," which literally means "smitten in conscience." Their response was, "What are we to do?" Peter replied, "Repent, and each of you be baptized … and you will receive the gift of the Holy Spirit" (NASB). Light came into their consciences, and glorious salvation followed!

Pause and Reflect

Have you noticed in yourself a tendency toward an either overscrupulous or a dulled conscience? What are some ways this false voice expresses itself in you?

Bring that to the Lord right now. Invite him to come and work in you to set things in order.

How The Conscience Develops

This structure of our souls develops when we are very young. It forms as we watch our parents respond to situations, and as we internalize our experiences with them. This is also true of the development of our consciences.[52] Loving nurture is the building block for developing a mature conscience. To the extent that our parents are healthy and nurturing, we take in what is good. But if our consciences are not fostered by loving nurture, they can become either overscrupulous or dulled.

A dull conscience in adulthood can be caused by lack of training and cultivation in childhood. A child who has not been trained by loving correction simply does not develop a healthy conscience. The conscience has not been awakened and shaped in clear ways, thus hindering ongoing development.

Some of us were brought up in discipline and instruction that was punitive and were shamed into a performance mindset. Anything unhealthy in our parents' attitudes, behaviors, expectations, or relationships

---

[52] Menninger, *Whatever Became of Sin?*, 22.

got absorbed and internalized. As a result, our neurotic (disturbed and reactive) conscience now warns us that we will be punished if standards aren't met, causing us to strive and perform. For example, a Christian may have a daily devotion time in an attempt to feel worthy and loved by God or do the right things as a way to attain God's favor.

A child can carry deep shame, and there are still times I hear my conscience saying many "shoulds": *you should have done it right; you should have done more; you shouldn't have done that; you should try harder.* It's a fear of punishment, a fear of being shamed. I don't want to fall short in some way and be found out. That's the old echo of adaptive performance from childhood. I have to quiet that old shaming voice, inviting the Holy Spirit to fill my thoughts with truth, love, and real conviction.

When our consciences become rigid, we often can't sense God's presence as a loving, nurturing presence. The unhealed conscience keeps circulating the "should" misbeliefs we haven't outgrown—*you should be ashamed; you should know better.* Children who were deprived of acceptance, nurture, and affirmation are still internally pleading for justice, and yet their conscience is covering up that need. And they are also covering up the anger from such deprivations. A child may have been told, "Be good, and don't be mad!" We absorb that message, hiding our anger, and creating an inner law that then governs our souls. We don't just need our shame healed; we need the shame-producing activity of our anxious consciences healed.

The good news is that God can wonderfully touch and comfort these early deprivations. Then when the Holy Spirit convicts us by bringing us to an understanding of our sins or errors that dishonor God, that conviction is clear and clean—there is a true remedy in the cross and our hearts can be at peace again.

Pause and Reflect

Would you take a few moments and with the Spirit's help remember any situations in your childhood that have contributed to a dulled or overly scrupulous conscience? What messages did you receive, and what patterns have emerged now in your behavior? Write those out and bring them to the Lord.

The Grace of the Cross

Ephesians 2:4–5 declares, "God, who is rich in mercy, because of His great love with which He loved us, even when we were dead in trespasses, made us alive together with Christ (by grace you have been saved)" (NKJV). By God's grace we have been forgiven yet we may find it difficult to receive that forgiveness. We often don't know how to take in and absorb the reality that he is faithful and just to forgive our confessed sin and to cleanse us from it (1 Jn 1:9). We aren't standing in the blessing that we have been pardoned for our rebellion and sin. We may confess the same sin repeatedly because our consciences keep bringing it up.

Why does this happen? Because our consciences are still operating under their own inner laws of right and wrong, untouched by the work of the cross. That old code binds us because we are still trusting in our own righteousness, our own way to be justified.

We may feel hopeful when we do well but then harsh with ourselves when we fall short. Striving like this keeps us living under the law. We have a desire to be good, but it is a "passion to be perfect" on our own.[53] We seek validity, worth, approval, and significance, a sort of security that comes from living within our own contrived standards. But violating those standards can foster much self-criticism, which doesn't help us not to feel guilty.

We need healing to learn to live under grace. The enemy uses our awareness of past sins to keep us bound to our identity with that sin. But that is no longer who we are and we no longer have to identify with our past mistakes. We are not our sins; we are not our past; we are not our wrong choices. Our inner law can cultivate self-hatred and a constant sense of shame. The antidote is to bring this to the cross, because at the cross there is no compulsion, no shame, and no condemnation. None. Jesus offered his body for us and now we're cleansed and sanctified.

We are to love ourselves well. But the old code written within us is not about love; it's a bondage the Lord wants to release us from. Sometimes we need to put a stake in the ground and say aloud, "This sin is completely forgiven!"

---

[53] Payne, *Restoring the Christian Soul Through Listening Prayer*, 143.

The vibrant Christian life depends on having a true sense of what God is like: He is good, holy, loving, merciful, kind, and ready to forgive. Yet in our souls we can be confused, unconsciously believing that God is like our own neurotic consciences rather than the giver of grace and righteousness.

I used to have a heavy cloud over me that would come and go—a sense of unease, feeling as if I could never do enough, or that I couldn't get things right. I had taken in rather harsh correction from my father, and then self-managed to reduce my anxiety. I tried to get it right in my own strength, and I did a lot of coping and performing. To come out of that striving I had to truly repent from the sin of pride that had taken root long before I knew what I was doing. In the power of the cross, I realized I needed to forgive my parents and release any judgments I held against them. I understood that it was the deprived child within me believing that, "My way is hidden from the LORD, and the justice due me escapes the notice of my God" (Is 40:27 NASB). In those deep places, I was unknowingly hostile to the Lord for the circumstances of my life and for always feeling the dread of punishment.

As I prayed over this situation one day, Psalm 131 came to mind. I understood that, as a secure child rests against a nurturing mother, so I could rest against the Lord. My imagination took in that picture, that reality. I could let him be my strength of conscience, my internal righteousness, so that I was quieted, free, and strengthened. He is my justice. He will bring everything around right in the end, filling my deprivations. Many times since then I have returned to that symbol and have chosen to rest in his righteousness when shame threatens to creep in.

When we repent over our interior processes the conscience receives healing. We can really know the Lord's forgiveness and gift of righteousness and have authentic conviction. The Holy Spirit is pinpoint specific when he brings conviction. We can ask, and he will faithfully show us any sin or complex of sins that requires repentance. Fr. Jacques Philippe wrote, "It is necessary that we know how to distinguish true repentance and a true desire to correct our faults. … The Holy Spirit does not inspire all of the reproaches that come to our conscience! … The feelings that come from the Spirit of God can be extremely powerful and profound, nonetheless, they are always peaceful."[54]

---

[54] Jacques Philippe, *Searching for and Maintaining Peace* (Staten Island, NY: ST PAULS, 2002), 63.

We can move from shame and condemnation to freedom, the freedom of loving obedience to God. The antidote to walking in our own internal laws is to walk in the Spirit, trusting Christ's righteousness alone, fully appropriating his cross so that we are at peace with God. We can wear the breastplate of his righteousness over our hearts (Eph 6:14). Only the Lord can "make the clean out of the unclean" (Job 14:4 NASB).

Our own consciences need to know that sin matters and has been answered for. Once our guilt is confessed, "the possibility of radical reformation opens up."[55] Christ's victory on the cross was God's answer to meet the demands of his own holiness. God was pleased to offer up his own Son to satisfy the demand of sin. Jesus was bruised and punished for our iniquities. Our consciences are cleansed and quieted by the cancellation of our guilt. Formerly alienated, we are now fully reconciled to God (Col 1:20–22). And made fully clean. John says simply that he "loves us and released us from our sins by His blood" (Rv 1:5 NASB).

Pause and Reflect

Once you have confessed your sin, are you in the habit of pausing to receive that forgiveness and thanking him for the cross, which alone cleanses you? Will you consider making that part of your spiritual discipline—the habit of truly receiving forgiveness and refusing to continue to strive about your sin? This is part of humbling yourself and recognizing him as your righteousness.

Paralyzing Shame

Sometimes shame paralyzes us. Shame and regret can stick around a long time after we have tried to deal with something. Perhaps we repeatedly confess that particular sin.

Shame operates like a powerful shadow government co-opting authority over our consciences. It works in the background, directing our souls at a deep level, isolating us, dismantling and undermining our walk of faith. The only answer to such shame is our confidence in Christ's righteousness.

---

[55] Menninger, *Whatever Became of Sin?*, 195.

Grace is the predator of shame. We simply confess our sins to the Lord and lean into him. Then, after receiving forgiveness for all that's confessed, we take in his grace, forgiving ourselves as well. In receiving forgiveness, we are putting on Christ, taking in his very righteousness. He is with us and within us. When we practice his presence, he is making us new.

This is how we are freed from the striving to become "good enough." We don't have to keep our sins constantly in mind, swimming in waters of shame and condemnation. When condemnation and shame come calling, we are able to say, *I stand in Christ alone; his righteousness is now mine.*

Our striving won't move us forward but collaborating with the grace of God's Spirit will. We can "choose to be led by the Spirit and so escape the erratic compulsions of a law-dominated existence" (Gal 5:18 MSG). The Spirit can speak and make everything else be still. Even if our consciences condemn us, "God is greater than our heart" (1 Jn 3:20 NASB).

Prayer for Healing

You are one with Christ. Acknowledge that now as you invite him to fill you and heal the voice of your conscience. Read Psalm 139 (especially verses 1 and 23–24) and invite the Lord to search and examine you.

Where your conscience has been malformed by the sin of another, pray in this way:

I forgive those who have defiled my conscience by their sin, or who created an atmosphere of shame, displeasure, reproach, and performance that shaped my soul. I forgive those who didn't nurture and help me develop a healthy conscience. (Name these.)

I release any irrational or inauthentic standards placed within me in my upbringing. Lord, touch and comfort these early deprivations so that I may be at peace. Where I am deprived of nurture and where I am still pleading for justice, I bring this to you. I forgive and release any anger or hostility into the cross. I trust you to bring justice.

Lord, establish order in me. Help me distinguish true guilt from false. Shrink the overscrupulous conscience that still strives. (With the eyes of your heart, see him do this.)

I receive the truth described in Isaiah 53:5–7: Jesus was pierced for my transgressions, crushed for my iniquities, chastened for my well-being, and scourged so I could be healed. My iniquity and my oppression were taken up in him as he was in anguish on my behalf. Thank you for this. Restore me, Lord, so I'm able to experience true guilt, repentance, and forgiveness.

If your conscience has been dulled or defiled, pray in this way:

I repent of any ways I have dulled my conscience through sin, through striving, performance, pride, introspection, or any artificial law I have organized my life around. Search and uncover these things, Lord.

Awaken in me a true conscience, alive in your Spirit and healthy. For those places in my soul that have grown dull or weak, for any way I have dishonored or bypassed my true conscience, forgive me and bring me into your light. Awaken in me those sleeping places.

Rebuild my gates as I choose to obey you, Lord. Shape and form my conscience and lead me into wholeness and truth. Align my conscience with my will, emotions, mind, intuition, desires, and imagination. May every part of me be in harmony.

Lord Jesus, come and move in my conscience so that this part of me—the guard and protector of my soul—will be ordered, awakened, and enlivened by your Spirit.

If you struggle with legalism:

Lord, help me let go of the internal laws I live in. Make them clear to me, Lord, and show me how I am to move forward. Release me where I've been trapped in the early years when I did not feel a loving presence but instead felt such shame. Heal me to live under grace and not laws.

Thank you for how you have made me, and for how I can learn to walk with you. You are rich in mercy! You are rich in forgiveness! You cover me in your righteousness. Bring me out of ignorance and instruct my conscience. Enable me to live by grace and freedom. Help me to protect and nurture my conscience by choosing the holy.

Homework

Name to the Lord any sin on your conscience and then pause to receive his forgiveness. Say aloud: *I am forgiven, I receive that deeply. Thank you, Lord, that you provided for my forgiveness in the cross.* Practice this often.

Recap

The conscience is the guard and protector of our souls, but can be malformed and become overly scrupulous or dulled. As the Lord brings understanding and healing to our consciences, we are renewed in our ability to walk in freedom, loving obedience, and grace.

In Part 1 we have looked at the voices of knowing and choosing—the will, the rational mind, the intuition, the imagination, and the conscience. Now let's turn our attention to Part 2, the Voices of Energy and Motivation—emotions, desires, and appetites.

PART II
VOICES OF ENERGY AND MOTIVATION

6

EMOTIONS

Purpose of Emotions

The origin of the word emotion is from the Latin *emovere,* which means "to stir, to disturb, to move out, or to move through." To experience emotions then, is to have inner movement.[56] God designed us to express our emotions in healthy, reflective ways and to enjoy a full life of properly ordered and energized emotions. Emotions form an essential and beautiful living energy of the soul, like a river continually changing its course. We need a structure to channel the river, and that is our souls.

The voice of our emotions is: *I'm stirred,* or *I'm moved by.* The false alternatives are to be either unmoved, stoic, and repressed, or neurotic and overly emotionally expressive in our reactions. If we weaken this voice because of repression, we become ill within, unable to access our emotions and to be moved by them appropriately. Then emotions will find a different means of expression, such as physical illness. Or we can get stuck in one emotion such as anger or sadness.

Conversely, if we passionately express all our emotional reactions, we will create confusion and destruction and stay in immaturity. We need to be brought back to the truth of how we are created and how to express emotions well and in complement with the other parts of our souls.

The movement of emotions gives us a sense of being alive and gifts us with lots of intuitive information. Our emotions move us or cause us to be moved toward something, and we respond with joy or sorrow, elation

---

[56] Judith MacNutt, lecture at School of Healing Prayer Level III, Nov. 2–6, 2009.

or disappointment, or any of the other primary and blended feelings, reactions, and sensations. Many researchers agree that there are at least eight primary emotions hardwired into the brain, and each has a polar opposite. These emotions are:

- anger;
- anticipation;
- disgust;
- fear;
- joy;
- sadness;
- surprise; and
- trust.

Others add shame, guilt, contempt, and awe. These core emotions can be combined and blended to derive a wide variety and range of feelings. A recently completed five-year survey of 7,000 people identified eighty-seven emotions but, surprisingly, people generally only recognize three primary emotions as they are experiencing them: sadness, happiness, and anger.[57]

Every emotion in its proper place can be a true expression of our souls when we are moving toward maturity. We tend to see emotions as negative or positive, like anger or joy, but all are appropriate and valid if they are expressed productively.

For instance, anger is a normal response to a frustrated goal or to injustice, but it can be disproportionate to the situation. Anger can motivate us to correct injustice or address a situation, but apart from the Spirit, anger can take over and turn into rage and bitterness. Anger may also protect us from a more vulnerable emotion like shame, grief, or fear.

Fear arousal can help us face or escape danger but can also descend into chronic anxiety, a fearful disposition. Like a warning light that stays in the on position, fear can become a default.

Grief is a cleansing emotion that allows stress relief when tears are shed but can turn into the heaviness of depression if repressed and unprocessed.

---

[57] Brené Brown, *Atlas of the Heart* (New York: Random House, 2021, OverDrive ebook edition), 43.

Persistent toxic emotions are warning signals—like flashing red lights—that something is amiss. Often these intense emotions come from unresolved experiences such as grief, abandonment, or trauma that keep trying to find a means of expression and a way out, demanding relief. We need to pay attention to these and ask the Holy Spirit what is amiss. He is always faithful to show us what is crooked. We don't have to default to a contaminated belief: *Oh, something is wrong with me because I have these feelings.*

Emotions are interior reactions to stimuli from an internal thought or an external experience. We are responding to an event, a perception, or a memory. Emotions are responses, not the source itself. Often, we believe they are originators, but they are like thermometers, not thermostats. A thermometer measures and indicates temperature or temperature gradient, but it does not set and regulate the temperature as a thermostat does. The thermostat activates the system to adjust when the temperature reaches a certain point.[58]

We should not ignore the thermometer but rather notice the specific emotion and its strength of response. Then we let the thermostat, which is the will, determine if an adjustment is needed. For instance, your child has left an assigned chore undone (yet again) and you feel irritation of some kind, perhaps anger or even disgust. That is a measurable response. How angry are you feeling? Where you allow that response to take you becomes the issue. Do you choose to express it in a productive way by setting appropriate consequences or let it emerge in disproportionate ways that wound your child?

The ability to regulate our emotions is an indicator of our health; the inability to manage our emotions is an indicator of immaturity and is associated with many mental health diagnoses such as anxiety, depression, substance abuse, and low impulse control.

Some indications of our emotional maturity are the developing ability to:

- feel, identify, and express our own emotions in healthy ways;
- take responsibility for our own emotions;

---

[58] Waterman, "Capacities and Motions of the Soul."

- set healthy boundaries;
- express real needs in a positive, assertive way with safe people;
- hold a clear value/belief system without being dogmatic;
- move forward with decisions and desires despite fear and criticism;
- respond to change and stress with resiliency rather than rigidity;
- feel anger and be assertive and productive rather than destructive;
- be humble and aware of our own weaknesses, admit wrongdoing, and verbalize an apology;
- live without undue shame, false guilt, or a hyperactive conscience;
- be aware of our own biases and refrain from expressing every opinion;
- deal with disappointment without going into prolonged depression;
- modulate heightened emotions and come back to balance;
- grieve well, integrating and accepting loss;
- seek help for prolonged emotional states such as anxiety and depression;
- initiate action instead of being a victim and blaming others;
- be intentionally vulnerable at appropriate times and receive support;
- show empathy and care for others and ourselves;
- feel empathy toward others without getting lost in their emotions;
- receive feedback without undue reactivity;
- recognize where we are privileged or gifted and use it well;
- work to develop effective communication skills to honor self and others;
- work to resolve conflict calmly;
- take responsibility for our own decisions, growth, and destiny;
- contribute to the growth of others; and
- separate from our family-of-origin appropriately to "become an inner-directed adult."[59]

---

[59] Peter Scazzero, *Emotionally Healthy Spirituality* (Grand Rapids, MI: Zondervan, 2006, 2017), 60.

Pause and Reflect

Did anything in the list you just read stand out to you (perhaps several things)? Is the Holy Spirit underscoring areas that he wants to cultivate in your soul? If so, pause now, write each one down, and commit each of those areas to him, naming your lack, your need for development, and your dependence on him to do the work within you. Take time with this and ask him if there are any specific ways he wants you to proceed.

Emotions and Thoughts

Emotions and thoughts are inseparably linked, operating in tandem. We need to have right thoughts in order to have appropriate emotions. Distorted thinking that originates from deeper governing beliefs and painful memories yields distorted emotions. Our thoughts feed our emotions. In fact, thoughts, judgments, perceptions, and experiences all inform our emotions. These can be magnified by personal history and relational pain. Emotional responses are indicators of our deep beliefs, giving voice to what's really going on in our souls. And if we are immature, we simply give in and live in the grip of these moods that have long been conditioned in us, unable to listen to reason. Our imaginations reinforce the intensity of the emotion. We stay subjective, overly sensitive, and untrained to choose well.

God has placed within us what we need in order to come out of subjectivity and immaturity so that we can change and be transformed in our emotional responses, able to be more objective. We can cultivate healthy emotions by his grace. Emotions are meant to serve a purpose, stirring and moving us, but are to be part of the whole harmony of our souls, submitted to our wills. While emotions are essential, they are not the true center we live from. To understand this is essential to our well-being.

If we live out of mere feelings, we will find ourselves unstable and unable to withstand suffering, temptation, and confusion. Our emotions may demand to be satisfied and justified, and thus end up controlling us. When emotions are allowed the primary place in our souls, all sorts of chaos will follow. Giving emotions pre-eminence is idolatry, the worship of the false, immature self. We need to recognize that we can stop tolerating and bowing to dark emotions. Willard expressed this well: "Feelings are good servants. But they are disastrous masters."[60]

We also need to recognize the place of emotions in addictions. Some pain, anxiety, or deadness inside of us makes us seek exhilarating feelings to distract us from pain and to give us a different reality. The "high" of these strong feelings becomes addictive. Then the addiction, which is a feeling phenomenon, gets a powerful grip on us. To break the grip of an addiction requires a willingness to deal with the emotional responses as well as the addiction itself.

Emotions and Faith

Sometimes the church has overemphasized or underemphasized the place of emotions. When overemphasized, the necessity of feeling the presence of the Lord is promoted. While the Lord does often meet us this way and we do engage him with our senses, scripture clearly exhorts us to live by faith, not by sensation. We are to live not by highs, but by depth. It is dangerous to demand or seek emotional experiences when pursuing the Lord, and an orientation toward doing so can invite the demonic. Emotions, when overemphasized, can pull us into the subjective and reduce reality to what we can feel in that moment.[61]

When we rely too much on emotions—waiting for the emotion to come first so that we can believe God's love—we can mistake shallow emotionalism and excitement for deep spirituality. But we need to learn to believe the Lord no matter the emotion, movement, or experience. We are to walk by faith, live by faith, and step into his love and truth no matter how we currently feel. We learn that something more than mere emotion is taking place: his Spirit really is moving within us!

On the other hand, the church can teach repression of feelings, considering them unimportant. The idea is to "just live by faith" and ignore emotions. But this is living without our full humanity. Imagine worshiping God with a blank face and a stiff posture, our emotions unengaged. We

[60] Willard, *Renovation of the Heart*, 122.
[61] Waterman, "Capacities and Motions of the Soul."

82

need to engage all our senses and live fully alive emotionally, managing our emotions well, and growing in our choices to mature.

Need for Objectivity

Emotions live within the images and memories we have stored internally. When memories are packed with symbols associated with strong feelings, these emotions hold "truth" for us, at least our perception of truth.

Many of us have learned to make decisions based on feelings. Wendy Backlund wrote: "Emotions don't validate truth; they validate what we believe. Our emotions are always affected by what we perceive as reality."[62] We live out of our emotions more than we know, which keeps us immature and trapped. Our decisions should be based in truth, rather than dominated by feelings that should be serving us.

"Most of us have been quite successfully conditioned to determine truth through the filter of our feelings. … But emotions are *not* truth's vocal twin and feelings are not the litmus test for reality. Our emotions and feelings are simply reactions to our environment, circumstances, and perceptions. By nature, they are followers, and we place our souls in danger when we require them to take the lead. Truth, on the other hand, was born to lead."[63]

Emotions need to be true expressions reflecting reality. We need to learn to examine our emotional responses and detach from them where necessary, not giving them a place of pre-eminence. We can learn to embrace truth no matter how loudly our emotions are speaking in their own unhealed language! When we become more objective and less subjectively led by our emotions, we are less susceptible to misinterpreting or exaggerating the seemingly negative responses we may perceive from others.

---

[62] Wendy Backlund, *Victorious Emotions* (N.P.: Igniting Hope Ministries, 2017), 27.
[63] Chole, *Anonymous*, 73.

Pause and Reflect

What have you been taught about the place of emotions and faith? Were they under-emphasized or overemphasized? What about their relationship to the will? Do you recognize any distortions in the way you frame your emotional life and its importance?

Early Shaping of Emotional Life

Our emotional life begins to be shaped shortly after birth. "The child's basis for emotional sturdiness is formed during early infancy." The nurturing a child receives "from its birth through age three will determine the path of emotional development which will carry it through its life."[64] Healthy nurturing in the early years sets us up for healthy emotional development.

Our parents were early models of how to express emotions and whether emotions were welcomed or dismissed. Some people still feel guilty when they cry or express too much emotion because they were shamed as children for their emotional expressions. Some had parents who themselves were shut down emotionally, therefore repression was learned and became an internal habit. Or a parent was emotionally dramatic and chaotic, and the child learned that emotions can't be controlled, that there is no real possibility to live in deep peace. Some have experienced so much anger, reactivity, and emotional instability in their family-of-origin that they are unable as adults to manage difficult emotions.

Early modeling tells us whether we can have healthy emotional boundaries with others. When we can't differentiate our own emotions from those of others, or when we have been taught to be too responsible for others, we may end up stabilizing for the sake of others, hiding our own emotional needs yet feeling quietly desperate. This often happens in chaotic families-of-origin or when our parents are too needy themselves to give us what we need. But there will come a time when we must deal with our own emotional needs. As adults, we may need to learn to distinguish our emotions from others' emotions. This takes wisdom, time, the help of others, and patient practice.

---

[64] Ryan, *Healing the Hidden Self,* 54.

In some unhealthy or toxic families-of-origin the chaos taught us that our emotions would be dominated by others. This leaves our emotional life underdeveloped, and we may believe our emotions can't be trusted to reflect reality. By prayer, we may need to be released from the diseased parts of our parents we have inherited or absorbed. Many of us need to learn to feel and name our feelings. We can sit with the Lord and ask him to help us do this. We can also do exercises in learning to feel and then express healthy emotions. Sometimes when we haven't had healthy models, we may need good books, a counselor, or a life coach to help us learn how to name our emotions and shape our responses. By applying ourselves to grow in this way, we can learn to read the signposts and make different choices. This is an essential part of our healing. Our emotions sometimes insistently tell us we have no choice in our responses. But we do have choices, and our freedom and transformation depend on learning to make wise choices in the expression of our emotions.

Pause and Reflect

How were emotions expressed in your family-of-origin? Was there room for every person in the family to have and express emotions? Did your parents model the healthy expression of emotions and teach you the same? Did one parent, more than the other, provide healthy emotional modeling? Where were the areas of lack? Can you identify where you have felt emotionally repressed or where your emotions have felt too chaotic and out-of-bounds?

Repression and Denial

Sometimes we repress feelings because they are so painful at the time the event happens. But repressed feelings that have not been processed and grieved do affect and trouble us in other ways, and we don't always make the connection with the original injury. If we ask, God will be faithful to raise the memories and issues we need to address. Choosing to feel pain is critical to our healing. We can trust him with any fear that this might be too painful. Defending ourselves by pushing emotions away is self-protection that only strengthens them at a deeper level. Our souls become silent with excessive grief or anxiety. We have to be willing to feel, to do the work of grieving, so that we can integrate our losses, and let the Lord bring up any repressed emotions and memories.

When we stay in apathy, the starvation of emotions, we have decided that it is just too costly to care, to connect, or to relate. Because we had pain and disruption at one time, we have withdrawn in a self-protection called "defensive devaluation." We devalue love and trust in order to protect ourselves from further pain, but this only causes the pain of isolation from others. Not to allow God-given emotions to move us in the right direction is sinful and brings "dis-ease" within ourselves and within relationships. God created us to be appropriately passionate and expressive, and not to shut down or over-modulate our emotions.

Denial of emotions is our unwillingness to accept things as they really are, even convincing ourselves of another reality: "I'm not really upset." But we are! We need to give ourselves the permission that God gives us to use the gift of emotion, the capacity to be moved with feelings. We need not deny emotions or even repress them, but instead recognize, interrupt, and replace destructive feelings or subordinate and channel them in a way that transforms their effects. As we begin to take responsibility for our own emotions, we begin to grow and see new possibilities.

Where we are unable to express feelings, emotions begin to build, and the repressed emotions cause us to become dysfunctional in some way. We cannot choose to have some emotions such as real joy, without having others. Emotions are like a circuit and if one link in that circuit is not permitted to function, all are affected. We may choose not to have pain, but then we don't feel deep joy either. We can't repress painful emotions and expect to be able to live in joy; we are created to have all emotions.

In our spiritual formation, feelings must be renovated. New ones must be encouraged, installed, connected, and heightened. For instance, if we have been taught that anger is sinful, we never learned how to express it well, and must now learn how to name and express anger appropriately. If we have used our anger in aggressive or passive-aggressive ways, learning to be respectfully assertive is our task. We often have to learn in our adulthood to find names and expressions for the emotions that weren't welcomed by our parents. Where we have hidden or disowned our own hearts, we need to welcome that disenfranchised part of our souls back and invite the Lord to restore and heal as he has promised to do.

Jesus Our Model

Jesus is our model, the human face of God. In his personhood he fully functioned emotionally, as should happen. His humanity gives us such hope. He is not disconnected from our humanity in any way. He knows what we're made of—our temptations to either repress emotions or let them crookedly dominate us—and he shows us the way. He can make the crooked places straight (Is 45:2).

We can explore his humanity, taking it in as our own. The Word came among us as man with a full emotional life. He expressed emotions well without defensive self-protection and hiddenness and without undisciplined passions. He was touched by and sympathized with our weaknesses while being "tempted in every way, just as we are" (Heb 4:15 NIV).

Scripture shows us that Jesus felt anger, grief, disgust, sadness, anguish, disappointment, joy, tenderness, trust, abandonment, and amazement. He took on the human condition and lived with his heart and emotions fully open. We are created in his image and likeness and must allow his humanity to come into our being. He was like us in every way, yet without sin, and is our model of the fullness and beauty of emotions felt, managed, and expressed well. In fact, we can pray: "Let your emotions enter me, Jesus."

Renovating and Ordering Emotions

Daily we are called to follow Christ and die to the old self. Dying to the old, false self does not mean that we kill our emotions, but that we put them to "death" by bringing them into their proper place, ordered and sanctified by the Spirit. Emotional maturity is managing emotions so they reflect variety and expression, yet don't dominate and control.[65]

---

[65] Waterman, "Capacities and Motions of the Soul."

By the Spirit's empowering, we can educate and train our feelings. We can learn to acknowledge them before the Lord, then move forward. We realize what we are feeling, but we don't stay in our feelings; we step into the truth and live there. This takes the enabling grace of the Holy Spirit, and time and patience with ourselves to change the old ways and cultivate the new ways. As we increase in emotional health and seek the Lord, we begin to see that the Holy Spirit is enabling us to know the power of an authentic life in Christ.

An example of this is my journey out of depression, which had afflicted me for many years. I wasn't emotionally healthy because my underlying belief system wasn't strong, clear, and steadfast. I wavered in my identity and my focus and was often double-minded because of my instability. And I gave significant credence to "my" depression, thus by agreement empowering it even more. I rehearsed my pain, romanced it, retained self-pity in it and felt like a powerless victim. It all seemed so true. I was the victim in my story, the lead actor in my narrative of depression.

In "my" depression, I entertained a lot of regret and self-pity. Then I felt drained by depression, anxiety, and hopeless thoughts, which stifled my growth. My core beliefs were laden with destructive thoughts and emotions. My brain followed suit by forming neurological loops that kept taking me back to toxic thoughts, which then provoked distorted emotions. I was recently looking in my old journals and found a mention of my struggle with depression more than 40 years ago. Members of my family, in two generations on both the paternal and maternal sides, have struggled with depression and mental illness, so it was an easy emotional slide for me to succumb to melancholy.

One day I awoke and told the Lord that I was feeling depressed, as usual, and would he please lift this from me? He spoke to me that day very simply and directly in a new way: "You don't have to be depressed." I wondered if I was really hearing the Holy Spirit. Did he just say that to me? But I was hearing and he was speaking! He began to show me how to take responsibility for the feelings of victimization underlying my depression, how to acknowledge the feeling but refuse to let it flood my system, and how to walk in a way that renewed my mind. I refused to hold others accountable for my happiness or give undue attention to depression, choosing joy and peace instead. In this way, depression began to decrease in frequency, duration, and intensity.

I love this exhortation when emotions threaten to overwhelm me: "Fitting every loose thought and emotion and impulse into the structure of life shaped by Christ" (2 Cor 10:5 MSG). Sometimes our emotions are erratic and would dominate us, but what we meditate on, we become, and we can meditate on the Word and be led of the Spirit. His Word, taken in over time, will change, correct, and reshape our emotions. When we learn to take care of the toxic, lie-laden thoughts and imaginations which disable us, we can reset our minds on Christ. Healthy emotions will follow.

Healthy emotions spring from a renewed mind, one in which we are structuring our deep beliefs around the love and the Word of God. It is our responsibility where we set our minds (Col 3:2; Phil 4:8), thus informing our emotions. Emotions are not the center of our being but are important in the structure of our souls and are intended to operate in harmony with our wills, minds, imaginations, and every part of us. As we live with Christ and in Christ he deepens and makes our true selves come alive with well-ordered emotions.

Prayer

First, give God the key to unlock your emotional life.

If your emotions are shut down, pray:

Lord, my emotions are repressed. I repent for where I've closed my heart down in self-protection or fear and created my own safety to manage the pain. I repent of any vow I've made to not feel in order to be safe. Forgive me for denying and repressing my emotions out of fear, for not living fully alive. Forgive me for not taking responsibility to manage my own emotions.

Please reactivate this part of my soul and call it into full being. I choose to feel, believing I won't be overwhelmed, but that you will accompany me on this journey of discovery.

If your emotions tend to swing or you feel you don't control them well, pray:

Lord, forgive me for living out of the idolatry of my emotions, for allowing them to dominate, hurting me and others. I repent of lies I have believed that I can't control my emotions. Your Word says that self-control is a fruit of the Spirit, so it is possible to control my emotions. I ask you to quiet the too-loud emotional voices. Thank you that my pain and sin were crucified on the cross with Jesus. I now receive your forgiveness, I take it in, and thank you. I forgive myself.

I forgive and release my mother, my father, and any other significant ones in my life who did not help me name and order my emotions well.

I forgive them for the harm of allowing their emotions to rule and dominate. Release me from the diseased parts of my parents that I have inherited or absorbed.

I forgive any who have caused me emotional trauma. (Stop and name them.)

Heal my emotional being, the colors and voices that are skewed and not reflecting truth. Lord, I ask you to come and set my emotions aright. Order them, Lord, as you heal my whole inner being. I want the voice of my emotions to be clear and strong and based in objective reality and your truth. I thank you that you want to be Lord of my emotions.

Set in balance all the voices of my soul and order my emotions with thoughts, will, conscience, imagination, desires, and intuition. Let your emotions enter and fill me, Lord Jesus. Help me develop the fruit of the Spirit in my emotional being, hearing your voice more loudly than any emotionally immature voices.

I receive your hope in this area. Teach me new ways step-by-step, choice-by-choice as I give attention to this area. Thank you that you want me to prosper and to enjoy emotionally healthy spirituality.

Renovate my heart that I may experience your goodness in this area.

Thank you that you have said (Ez 36:36 NASB): "... I, the Lord, have rebuilt the ruined places and planted that which was desolated. ..." Plant good things in my emotions. As you bring my emotions to life and order, cause your breath to enter that I may come fully alive (Ez 37:5 NASB). Cause me to know real hope, real joy, real peace, and experience real love. Thank you that I receive healthy and ordered emotions from you.

Homework

Earlier in the chapter, you read a list of the signs of emotionally mature development and identified areas of weakness in your emotional growth. As you name these before the Lord, what are specific ways you can move forward to develop each of these areas? The Holy Spirit will help you as you consider the need for honesty with and support from an accountability partner, mentor, or counselor.

The journaling exercise with "arrest, renew, cultivate" near the end of Chapter 2—The Rational Mind—will also be helpful here.

Recap

Emotions are an essential and beautiful living energy of the soul and we need to understand how we are created so that we can express emotions well and in complement with the other parts of our souls.

Emotions stir and move us, but they are not the true center we live from. We are to live by faith, and in the truth. By applying ourself to understand and take responsibility for our emotions, we can come alive with well-ordered emotions and experience transformation.

Now let's look at another energy of our souls, that of desire.

7

DESIRE

Desire is our great capacity to dream, hope, yearn, and aspire to that for which we dream. As a beautiful and powerful voice of longing, it calls us to live fully alive to our dreams. John Gaynor Banks wrote of desire as a "radiant thing," the "mighty force" that is "part of the atomic energy of the soul."[66] Banks said that the kingdom of heaven within us is activated and operated by desire.

All Christianity is an invitation to desire. And desires are intended to propel and move us forward toward fruitful, rich lives.

Orientation

To desire is a gift. Desires are deep waters within us, deep wells of energy. The issue is how they emerge. Since it takes a lifetime to be transformed into Christlikeness, how we manage our emerging desires is essential to that transformation. We must recognize our desires. We must reckon with them. We must listen to them and give them voice.

With our wills we choose to express and develop our desires, and with our character we shape them. Psalm 37:4 indicates that delight *in* the Lord is to come before we ask for our desires to be met: "Delight yourself in the Lord; And He will give you the desires of your heart" (NASB). This order is important because as we reach forward to attain our desires, if our

---

[66] John Gaynor Banks, *The Master and the Disciple* (St. Paul, MN: Macalester Park Publishing, 1954), 5.

character is out of order, we won't attain our desires with right hearts and that may harm us and others. Our delight in the Lord should orient and motivate all we do.[67]

Desires are influenced by our beliefs and our perceptions of reality. How we frame and perceive experiences comes into play as we consider how and what we desire. For instance, if I believe that there won't be enough for me then I'll hardly dare to believe that my desires should be pursued and could be fulfilled. If I believe I am inept in some way, I won't allow myself to pursue desires that require real effort.

Part of the journey of desire is a willingness to allow the Spirit to expose any toxic messages that hinder the pursuit of desires. Desires are inextricably tied to and shaped by our thoughts and beliefs. If we don't dare to desire, there is a misbelief within. Or if we desire but don't believe we are worthy to attain that desire, there is an underlying wrong belief. Our desires will line up under and reflect the truths or untruths that we believe.

As believers, our wonderful inheritance and call is to listen to the Lord. A. W. Tozer encourages us in this, that the Holy Spirit "takes the things of God and translates them into language our hearts understand."[68] Listening and taking in what God is conveying is key to moving forward with desires. And moving forward means we are taking responsibility for our destiny in the Lord; we are activating our wills to desire and orienting our emerging desires toward his will and ways. The will and desires work in tandem because a strong, active will is "animated by desire."[69]

Desires aren't the same as emotions, which can change with circumstances. Desires may emerge but be carried away on the winds of emotions. When excitement wanes, as it always does, we may abandon our desires. On the other hand, if we intentionally repress our emotions, we can stop our desires from flourishing. The process of naming and guarding our desires is essential to our spiritual development, as is the willingness to hold them before the Lord so that they can be refined and clarified over a lifetime. We must learn to retain and treasure our desires until he fulfills them in his way, in his time. We need endurance to wait for this. Discipline steadies, shapes, and anchors our desires, providing the space

---

[67] Waterman, "Capacities and Motions of the Soul."

[68] A. W. Tozer, *The Mystery of the Holy Spirit* (Newberry, FL: Bridge-Logos, 2007), 62.

[69] Jacques Philippe, *Interior Freedom* (Strongsville, OH: Scepter Publishers, Inc., 2007), 105.

for them to be expressed and flourish. We may have high aspirations, but our priorities, habits, character, and efforts must be matched by motivation so we can accomplish what we desire.

Sometimes we let dreams fall away prematurely because they are so much bigger than our resources. So, we don't dare to trust. But dreams are supposed to be more than we can understand and accomplish because God is the one at work within us. That's what the supernatural is about: the greater things, the things his Spirit can accomplish in and through us as we are in union with him (Jn 14:12). Our desires are part of the greater desires of God for his kingdom.

Pause and Reflect

Consider what you have just read about desire. Will you invite the Lord into your desires just now? If he has begun to identify any fears or reluctance on your part, will you write those out and bring them to the Lord? If you recognize that you have edited your desires out of self-protection or lack of hope, write that out.

Desire Greatly, Desire Strongly

Many of us are not in touch with our hearts' desires because we fear we might be disappointed. We may prefer to hide and be half-hearted, hedging against disappointment, instead of bringing our longings, indeed our whole capacity for desire before the Lord. In *The Weight of Glory,* Lewis wrote: "Indeed if we consider the unblushing promises of reward … it would seem that our Lord finds our desires not too strong, but too weak."[70] Our desires are not too strong but too weak!

God's desires for us are strong and he wants *our* desires to be strong. He wants to fulfill our desires with good things (Ps 103:5), grant us our hearts' desires (Ps 20:4; 21:2; Prv 10:24), and satisfy our desires in scorched places (Is 58:11). He really does want to bless and complete our desires. He created us with the capacity to want because we are created in his image,

---

[70] C. S. Lewis, *The Weight of Glory* (New York: HarperOne, 1949, revised 1980), 26.

in the image of a passionate, creative God. Thus, we can ask the Lord to fulfill our creative capacities.

When we are living from our hearts' desires, we feel his pleasure. We sense him at work within us "both to will and to do for *His* good pleasure" (Phil 2:13 NKJV). But sometimes we feel ashamed of our desires, usually an adaptive response from childhood, or fear that our desires are not in line with God's will. Sometimes our needs and desires feel shameful to us until we come to know how deeply accepted and loved we are, how welcome our needs and desires are. He encourages us to name our desires without shame and frustration, knowing every promise is yes and amen in him! We haven't truly taken in the profound generosity of our God. It is his good pleasure to help us shape and then grant us the desires of our hearts.

God, who designed us for his glory, gifted us with the capacity for deep desire. And we can direct our desires toward good or evil (Hos 4:8). Indeed, the person we are becoming is directed by desire. Tozer wrote: "Every Christian will become at last what his desires have made him. We are the sum total of our hungers. The great saints have all had thirsting hearts."[71] The psalmist echoed this thirst in Psalm 42:1 (NIV): "As the deer pants for streams of water, so my soul pants for you, my God." As Christ himself becomes our first and greatest desire, then our desires for all other things can become defined, ordered, well-directed, and whole.

Sometimes longing calls us in a new direction. We need courage to pay attention to this and act on it. The Holy Spirit can't wait for that next good and beautiful thing we create together with him, seeing our desires and his desires come together. He not only wants to fulfill the desires of our hearts, but he also wants to give us desires that are much bigger than us, that even scare us sometimes because we can't believe they might be something God would call us to. These may be the things described in Ephesians 3:20 that go immeasurably beyond all that we could think, ask, or even imagine. But he wants us to take hold of those things as well—pray into them, be pregnant with them, dare to believe.

---

[71] A. W. Tozer, January 8 reading in *Tozer on the Almighty God: A 365-Day Devotional* (Chicago: Moody Bible Institute, 2004, 2020).

Pause and Reflect

Are you willing to ask the Lord for desires that feel beyond what you can manage, think, imagine, and manufacture?

Ask the Lord if there is any block that causes you not to step forward in fervent desire. Write it out.

Desire Greatly, Desire Purely

Desire can have the true voice of longing but also a false voice of demand arising from the carnal self. We can turn desire into demand and craving when the longings become idolatrous. Instead of *I dream*, our voice becomes *I demand*. If our desires are fleshly, they will bring us suffering because unpurified desires become destructive. We find trouble when we let the demands of our desires drive us rather than choosing to regulate them.[72]

Our problems, addictions, and out-of-control appetites may be hiding true desires. We need to ask: what is that fleshly desire hiding that needs to be revealed? Sometimes our desires involve what we deeply want and see as good for another person. But then we may start trying to control another. In our prayers, we may even try to do this with God. Christians can fall into this trap when we have an agenda for our desires and expect others or God to fulfill them in our ways in our time.[73]

Sometimes our desires arise from deceit or illusion. When that happens, we may find ourselves in a place of exploiting or manipulating others in order to fulfill those desires. At this place, God's refining fires are a needed mercy. We see this in scripture when God journeyed with people such as Moses, Abraham, and Joseph, as well as Peter and Paul, through years of maturing until their desires could be fulfilled. He took them through the process of surrender, self-denial, and trust. How great is our need for maturity as we contend with the atomic power of desire!

One of the most chilling verses in scripture is the indictment against Israel in Psalm 106:15 (CJB): "He gave them what they wanted but sent

---

[72] John Mark Comer, *The Ruthless Elimination of Hurry* (Colorado Springs, CO: Waterbrook Press, 2019), 144.
[73] Waterman, "Capacities and Motions of the Soul."

meagerness into their soul." There is a carnal part of us that demands what it wants, and our souls suffer leanness because of it. It is the Spirit's work of sanctification that cleanses and purifies, differentiating between demand and desire. It is the Spirit who helps us see "when our desires are amiss, or simply not His chosen best for us."[74]

It is the Spirit who helps us to desire good things, to desire them in genuine ways, and to wait on the Lord. To mature we must die to our self-demanding ways and allow him to burn away the false. Some desires then simply blow away as ash, others come out purer, more tempered, but also larger and stronger.

We reckon with our desires by surrendering them to God. When Banks suggested that the kingdom of God within us is operated by desire, he went on to add: "Do not quench it or crush it … rather offer it to God."[75] We have a way of grace, to offer our desires to God as a living sacrifice (Rom 12:1–2). In offering them to God, we then keep surrendering the outcomes to God. Our desires need not be squashed, but submitted to God, re-formed within us by purification. We simply cannot bypass the process of surrender and self-denial, which creates greater humility and capacity in us.

The dross within our desires has to be taken away, and it must be by fire, so we actually feel the heat. When we want to run away from the fiery pain, we need to realize that the pain may be God's action in us to make our desires greater and purer. We may desire renown, ministry, relationships, career, or any number of other aspirations. Where the Lord is burning, we will either encounter him or run from him.[76]

Disappointment

When things don't go the way we think they should, often the root of what is being tested is our desires. We are tempted to fall into disappointment, which leads us to a sense of injury and offense, even depression, and we may try to hedge against it by simply not desiring and hoping. But he

---

[74] Payne, *Listening Prayer*, 78.
[75] Banks, *The Master and the Disciple*, 5.
[76] Waterman, "Capacities and Motions of the Soul."

knows how to set order into our souls even in the places of our unknown resistance and self-pity.

We may have desired a certain outcome, but God isn't just a God of outcome, he's a God of process, of transformation. We may obstruct our own expectancy to avoid being disappointed. Hopelessness can be a defense against really dealing with issues, against hoping in our real desires.

Depression and hidden misbeliefs suppress or take away our capacity to desire and diminish the will to move forward in our desires. We may experience the malaise of not knowing what to ask the Lord, or how to continue in hope. The enemy comes to steal our hope, but our birthright in the Lord is to abound in hope by the power of the Holy Spirit (Rom 15:13). Part of maturity is learning to deal with disappointments, learning not to let them turn into a sense of real injury and even the sin of prolonged despair.

Instead, we hurt but learn to grieve, adjust, and keep hoping in good things. We choose maturity, not victimhood. Adulthood means flexibility—modifying courses and making alterations so that desires stay alive as they are being sifted and purified. Otherwise, we can be crushed under the weight of suffering and give up.

Life can come wrapped in difficult, messy packages. But Paul tells us in 2 Corinthians 4:18 to look at the unseen eternal, not the temporary. Inside difficulties, God is giving us gifts. He turns ashes into beauty, deserts into blooms, and death into life. When we know how good he is, we can trust him to do that, to transform us and our desires as we persevere with him and find treasure in the darkness. God is a good, good Father and being convinced of that moves our healing along. He meets us in our intimacy with him. May he come and give us grace to lay down our defenses as he encounters us with his Spirit and Word.

Besides disappointment, another enemy of hopeful desire is the presumption that things should look the way I think they should, or I'll be deeply disheartened. This presumptive pride can creep in on us and turn into a cold, quiet anger with God that renders us passive.

But we have a beautiful capacity to choose and move toward hope. We have the goodness and mercy of a sovereign, faithful God streaming toward us. We can dare to hope, knowing he is at work even when we aren't seeing and recognizing what he's doing now. We must have an unshakeable conviction that he is always with us, he is faithful, and he will show up. We hope, but don't demand; we expect, but hold our hearts open to all possibilities. He has overcome and turned back our enemy; he is mighty, so we can take hold of his promises and soar into hope.

Pause and Reflect

Has the Holy Spirit identified for you any area where you have had an idolatrous demand? Bring that to him in repentance.

Ask him to show you any area of disappointment or hopelessness, perhaps buried, that he wants to deal with so that your desires can rise again. Write these out, including your emotions about them. Forgive others and yourself where necessary.

Ask him if there is any step you can take now in moving toward fulfilling your desires. Write that out so you can be accountable to step forward.

Invite him to cause you to thrive and flourish again.

Dying and Rising

Colossians 3:1–10 (NIV) exhorts us: "… You died, and your life is now hidden with Christ in God. … Put to death, therefore, whatever belongs to your earthly nature. … Put on the new self." How do we put our desires to death so that we can live in our true selves? Certainly not by killing them or neutralizing them, but by allowing God to test and purify them, sifting out what is not of him. If we submit to the Holy Spirit, the wrong things we desire fade, and the good desires remain and flourish.

We experience God's burning love as we die to self and live in this new way with him. We can agree to cooperate and invite his love to burn away the dross of distorted desires. Sometimes the old gets burned out and we don't even know what our real desires are; we have to wait for the Lord to give us new desires.

Sometimes "our souls may need to catch up with our longings." Our desires may be genuine, but "the soul needed to carry them may need to grow larger."[77] They are too weighty for our present immaturity. God wants good things for us, but we need to be able to carry and manage them. In his goodness, he keeps transforming us in preparation for those good things. Even when desires are fulfilled, we keep offering those to him as well, so they don't become idolatrous. By faith, Abraham offered up Isaac as his heart was being tested by the Lord, and God found Abraham faithful.

Pause and Reflect

Where is God burning and refining your desires? Will you welcome his purifying love, thanking him for his refining fire because it is the very thing you need in order to realize the greater things he has for you?

Recognizing and Recapturing True Desires

How can we discover or rediscover our desires? Our desires may be long buried, and we can choose to ask the Lord to uncover, heal, and place fire within us again. We need to find where God is stirring and burning, recapture the desires, name them, and also allow God access to our whole hearts. He wants to speak and lead through our desires.

I certainly experienced this when, in my early fifties, I began to pursue a PhD. This had been a long-buried desire from thirty years before that God poked, prodded, and resurrected. Even after he opened the door with a scholarship, the task seemed so daunting that I almost dropped out the second week. (How could I possibly expect to pass the orals, much less write a dissertation?) That week, a scripture given to me by my youngest daughter reminded me of the Lord's call to this dream, and I refastened my seat belt for the journey. Continued obedience and discipline gave shape to each class and the final hurdles of the exams and dissertation. During those four years I encountered numerous unexpected life challenges—a job change, cancer, divorce, my father's death, a move, my last child leaving home—but desire, the atomic energy of the heart, motivated by the Holy Spirit, kept burning, kept spurring me on to completion even in

---

[77] Waterman, *Songs of Assent*, 176, 178.

the difficulties. Sometimes I ran well, sometimes I stumbled, sometimes I stood still and just breathed, but by grace and the support of others I crossed the finish line.

Without desires, we are only half-alive. Fearing that our dreams will never be fulfilled, we may avoid laying out before the Lord our deepest desires. We may reason: "If I don't want too much, God won't disappoint me." This is a false voice of hopelessness. Instead of contending with the real content of our hearts in his presence, we cover and quench our desires, retreating into a self-imposed safe, silent zone.

But safety cannot be found by retreating into the false self. Our quest must be to boldly name our desires, trusting he will hold them safely as we look to him as our first desire. We aren't to give up in apathy, but we move forward, soaring in hope, realizing hardship is a true gift. God told Abraham to look up at the stars, so many are his hopeful promises. This is still our call.

What have you let go that you should not have? It's one thing to commit something to God and wait on him, another to simply give up. We want to stay childlike in our trust while we pursue maturity, retaining our curiosity about what a great big God can do. We must be willing to wake up from our deadness (Eph 5:14). The waking can be painful, but we must awaken and remain fully awake!

A friend of mine, who has allowed me to share her story, began to be awakened by the Lord to her heart's desires. During prayer, she had a short but life-defining memory. Married and in her twenties at that time with three little children, she and her husband had just purchased their first small home and she was thrilled with it. As she showed her dear grandmother around, her godly but duty-bound grandmother said: "And what are you doing for the community?" In that moment, her heart froze around the lie that she should not be taking such delight in her home, in the fulfillment of her desires. She "ought" to be placing her energy elsewhere, doing more for others.

Unknowingly, she took in that sinister message, squashed her desires, and in her forties had a sense of perplexity as to what she should be doing with her life. The compunction of conscience had dammed up her ability to dream and desire. But the Lord, in his wonderful grace and pursuit of her, began to awaken her to truth again, calling her to recapture her heart's desires.

She later wrote of this journey of desire, disappointment with God, and recapture of her dreams:

> I am a dreamer. Have been as long as I can remember. What I love about dreams and desires is their proclivity to impossibility, but that same proclivity paired with my expectation led me to a wilderness of disappointment. I was sure my desires would take the path I had neatly laid out for them in my imagination. I desired the dream over the dream giver, stomping down my own path, pulling Jesus along, and soon found myself deeply disappointed by the outcome. Jesus met me there, picked me up and asked if he could lead. As I followed, he began to repair, replace, and redeem.
>
> When I heard this teaching on desire, it resonated with me, and I suddenly realized I had gone from dreaming to apathy. The Lord took me by the hand and walked me to the truth, shined light on the lies and gently walked me through the truth of what purified desires look like. It is as if I have awakened from a deep slumber. I am dreaming again and discovering all of the desires hidden in my heart. I am so grateful for this restoration.

Like my friend, we may need to come free from lies and the legalism of an unhealthy conscience so God can grant our desires.

Sometimes religion has told us that to have desires is selfish, or that we must have only spiritual desires. We may need to give duty a rest and set aside some time to find out what we really want. We release control by surrendering to the Lord and worshipping, resting in him with our desires. Then we learn to pray that he will grant us our hearts' desires and fulfill all our plans (Ps 20:4). We keep longing, but from a place of abiding in him, welcoming his presence.

Thwarted Desires

To deeply desire and not attain our dreams can bring such pain because "hope deferred makes the heart sick" (Prv 13:12 NIV). When we begin to lose hope because of blocked desires, anger and despair can ensue. We can even shame and despise ourselves for hoping. We may have mistaken the desires of our hearts for the voice of God and adopted counterfeit desires. Or we may have mistaken the whispers of the enemy as our own desires. It takes time to recognize these things and adjust.

Sometimes thwarted desires result from God's delay, in which case we must wait with confident endurance. Sometimes we have to recognize where the enemy has hindered us so we can turn and withstand him. We may need to battle for our desires. The desires that are not yet fulfilled we commit to him because he is faithful.

The Lord knows when our character is ready to bear the weight of fulfilled desires. So, we ask him to help us keep collaborating with him and paying the price to come into fullness. And we take each small step he indicates to us.

When the energy of desire has diminished, it is by prayer that the flow of living water comes again to fill the well, reawaken creative dreams, and infuse us with momentum to pursue those desires aright. In our true selves, when we are quiet before him in listening prayer, he draws up the deep desires of our hearts, aspirations we may have quenched or set aside prematurely. As we pray, desires long repressed may emerge, so we capture them, write them out, and pray into them.

Then, as we acknowledge these desires, offering them to God so that our wills become his, we can listen to his word of healing and direction that sustains us until the time of fulfillment. Faith, united with enduring patience, remains the key to pleasing God and receiving our promised desires (Heb 6:12). He is able to do something great for his kingdom's glory and our fruitfulness!

In his presence, we must repent of self-willed, self-timed demands. We offer him our disappointment in waiting; we offer him our grieving and our double-mindedness over thwarted or quenched desires; we offer him our mistaken counterfeits and shaky attempts at self-fulfillment; and we open all the hidden places of our hearts to his light. Then, repentant, we return to hope and invite him to bring up and restore buried desires. We can sense anew the Holy Spirit's creative indwelling presence so willing to restore all within us "brimming with endless possibility," including deep desires.[78]

In faith we trust deeply that we can wait for that good thing we are asking because he is a good God, full of grace and lovingkindness toward us. He will be faithful to every promise. We turn again to that place of abiding in his presence, offering our desires in joy, being strengthened as we wait, inviting his purification, uniting with Christ who is greater than all our desires and has the power to open his hand and fulfill every good desire.

Prayer

Lord, I now give you access to my heart and to that deep capacity within me to desire and long, and to name and give voice and creativity to those specific yearnings. Thank you for this beautiful gift of desire—so rich and so scary—that calls me to something greater than myself.

Forgive me where I have let my desires fall away, where I believed wrong things, where I acted only out of duty, where I was so hurt that I slipped into apathy, disappointment, and even bitterness. Show me those places that I might offer them to you for healing. (Pause and give him time to show you.)

Where I have strived to fulfill my own desires, strived to even find them, forgive my striving that hindered your grace. Forgive my fears: fear of disappointment, fear that I won't pursue the right desires and will miss you or misuse what you have given, fear that I am not worthy to ask great things of you, fear that resources won't be available to fulfill my desires.

When I let my expectations of you wane, when my faith was diminished in your ability to meet me with your goodness, my heart became dull and apathetic. Forgive me, Lord, for my unbelief, my hesitancy to embrace my destiny because of my own limitations. In my scarcity I didn't see your largeness and fullness.

---

[78] Guardini, *The Lord*, 36.

Lord, sometimes I have let my longings become demands and then blamed you for the outcome. As you forgive and wash me, I choose to let my expectations soar again. I choose hope.

Lord, give me the will again to desire, and strengthen my will to sustain my desires. Those desires that I have pushed to the side that really are of you, I ask you to restore and strengthen. Grant me courage to pursue them.

I won't turn off my longing, even if it's painful. Help me face the pain and stay present. Let a flame burn within me again, not only for you, but for the things you have put in my heart to long for. May the force of your desires in me and for me tenderly come and awaken me.

Thank you for your purifying work. I want to collaborate with you, seeing you in the process. I ask you to purify and prepare me to carry the weight of the desires you have for me.

Things long forgotten I ask you to recall to my heart. Let dead, dry things come back to life. Restore and enliven my desires and my imagination. Rebuild all my waste places and plant any desolate places so that I may be cultivated and thrive.

I ask you to restore the desires I have let fall away. Redeem and breathe life again, Lord. And I ask you to place new desires within me as you burn the old away. Let me dream with you.

You want me to believe that you will grant my heart's desires and fulfill all my plans (Ps 20:4). Thank you for this promise as I arise to believe. I look to the stars in the night sky and my hope soars. Lord, watch over your word to perform it (Jer 1:12).

May I continue always to burn with desire for you even when I don't understand what's happening in my circumstances. May I give you first place in my longings. May I always wait on you and thirst for you.

I pray for the same heart as Jesus when he said: "I delight to do your will, my God" (Ps 40:8 NASB). I pray you will keep alive within me your most precious gift—a burning longing for you.

Homework

Are you willing for the Lord to reopen your heart to your long-buried desires? As he does, write those out and purpose not to let them fall away again, but to pray, battle, and prepare for them. Keep this as a section in your journal that you continue to update. (Keeping a spiritual journal with a section for your desires is an important practice in trust, in keeping alive the dreams, and in keeping them before the Lord.)

Recap

Desire is a mighty force within our souls, a force that needs to be recognized, oriented, purified, surrendered, and strengthened. We can recover our true longings and be fruitful in our desires as his Spirit enables us.

Now let's take a look at appetites, which are the connectors between the soul and the body.

8

APPETITES

Appetites are the connectors, the way the soul and the body intersect. Our bodies experience sensation through the eyes, ears, skin, nose, and mouth, and appetites engage all these bodily senses. Appetites are the energy of the body transferred into need: hunger, thirst, rest, sexual drives, exercise, and touch. These are legitimate needs that help us survive and thrive, express and enjoy life, connect with others, and take care of ourselves in healthy ways. Healthy appetites are like power supplies of energy that propel us forward in necessary and good ways.[79]

We need this propelling energy, but we don't want to be driven by it. Instead, we need to direct it. Think of a river, able to give such life. Our rivers, the bodily energies, need well-established banks in our souls to direct the life-giving flow and avoid destructive consequences.

Our physical being is an incredible gift, the creation of God who loves matter. Pope John Paul II affirmed that by creation there is a deep and constant association between our personhood and the way we live in our human bodies.[80] Because God is our Maker, we should consider how we are to live in our bodies with gratefulness and have a deep, sacred, courteous, dignified relationship with our bodies. Our bodies are good, and we need to make friends with them, care for them, and use them well for they are our instruments on this earth, in this place and time, for living well.

We see this in the life of Jesus. He came in a body and that body was vitally important to expressing God's nature on earth and releasing the

---

[79] Waterman, "Capacities and Motions of the Soul."
[80] Christopher West, *At the Heart of the Gospel* (New York: Image Books, 2012), 12.

power of God. And we are to be like him, which means the expression and use of our bodies in the present is vital. We are fearfully and wonderfully made, and when our bodies are inhabited by his presence, we house his grace and beauty. Such a privilege and a responsibility.

In Romans 12:1–2 Paul tells us to present our bodies as a living sacrifice to God as our reasonable worship to him. Then we are transformed by renewing our *minds* in him, rather than being conformed to the world's system and culture. Interesting that these two things—body and soul—are linked, and both are necessary for us to find, prove, and walk out God's will. The idea of presenting our bodies to God as part of the spiritual service of worship is key to understanding our part. In 1 Corinthians 6:19–20, Paul tells us that we have been redeemed, bought with the price of Christ's blood, enabling us to glorify God in our bodies, which are his temple. Such a singular thought: to glorify God in our bodies, not just our souls. Another translation says: "A price has been paid for you. So, make your body a showplace of God's greatness."[81]

Our whole being is a gift to us that we can offer back to him by how we live, glorifying him. Our choices in how we take care of our bodies and use them to express worship really do matter. We can use our bodies in unrighteous ways, or we can present our different bodily parts to him to be used as weapons of righteousness (Rom 8:13).[82] We don't tend to think in those terms, do we? But we can offer ourselves to God in this way and we can do so regularly. When we present our bodies and appetites to the Lord, this is an ongoing holy surrender. We keep offering ourselves to the Lord, renewing our minds, engaging our wills to choose against any sinful leanings and demands of the body, yielding to him. This is a living thing that we do, and we can make our bodies allies of our Christian walk. The energies of the body are to serve us; we are not to become slaves of our bodies.

Our bodies are our domain, so it is of vital importance that we take responsibility to govern and honor them and not let other inclinations dominate. Where our culture is sexualizing everything, where it is ashamed and afraid of aging bodies, where bodies are marred by abortion, where alcohol and drug addictions are common, we must be a people set apart,

---

[81] Willard, *Renovation of the Heart*, 159.
[82] Ibid.

making conscious choices regarding how we think about and treasure our bodies, how we express our appetites.

God loves and has created matter, but Satan hates matter and our bodies are matter. So, our enemy is going to try to distort and destroy what is of our bodies. We are inhabited by grace, yet we can carry a lot of body shame and hostility. Unless we genuinely love and accept ourselves, we are unable to fully accept our bodies as good and the enemy will use this shame in destructive ways.

The source of some autoimmune diseases may be this hostility toward ourselves, in which we agree with the enemy about our unworthiness or ugliness. This is why developing sincere self-acceptance is so vital to our well-being. We are influenced by our bodies, and they are influenced by our emotions, imaginations, thoughts, attitudes, and desires—an important interplay. Attitudes settle into our bodies—our body language, the nonverbal expressions we convey, how we hold ourselves, how we extend or withdraw touch to and from others, how we treat ourselves—are all expressions of our souls via our bodies. Others around us are more aware of what our own body is doing and saying than we know.

Voice of the Appetite

The voice of the appetite is *I need,* but appetites can intensify into *I demand* and develop strongholds or can be suppressed into a false *I don't need.* Our appetites can either serve us or erupt in harmful ways and take over as cravings and addictions that drive us. The river of our appetites channeled well helps us enjoy good things, because God created pleasure and wants us to experience enjoyment within safe bounds.

When our souls are not functioning appropriately, then an appetite such as hunger, sexuality, exercise, or sleep can flood and take over everything. The body's needs are sensory, so our temptations will be right there with food (including alcohol), sex, rest, even exercise. When we have abdicated our authority to these power sources, we can quickly spiral into gluttony, laziness, or addiction of some kind. The body, apart from grace, has its own agenda, which is a demand to experience pleasure and avoid pain.[83] Through appetites, Satan lures us with the temptation of immediate gratification.[84]

The enemy dupes us into acting as if we are victims of our own appetites. But this is not the truth. We really can bring them under control by self-governing and direct them to their proper place. We have a decision to make, and the heart of it is: what god will we serve and worship with our appetites? What god will we allow to claim us?

Pause and Reflect

Have you recognized that your body is a temple of God's Spirit, that you are not your own because you have been bought with the price of his blood? Have you thought of the need to be gracious and courteous to your own body? Perhaps, realizing this intersection of your body and soul, you would like to pause and commit your body again to the lordship of Jesus, repenting of any misuse of your body.

Food and Hunger

All creation is a sign and means of God's presence. Food is created and given by God as communion with God and celebration with others. When we allow food to be a sacrament to us, it makes God more known to us, and is an expression of his grace and provision. "O taste and see the Lord is good …" (Ps 34:8 NASB1995). But our food consumption can also be an expression of our loneliness and brokenness.

Many of us are not at home in our own bodies, and how we receive food, how we use food, reflects that. Some of us carry excess weight because we have never learned to form disciplined, healthy eating habits or because we are "eating our pain" or filling our boredom. For some, sugar addiction is "acceptable," but in our modern diseases medical research indicates that the inflammatory response in our bodies is linked to sugar. Hidden in our desire for sugar may be a sincere craving to experience

---

[83] Menninger, *Whatever Became of Sin?*, 28.
[84] Chole, *Anonymous*, 65.

the sweetness of life, of connections, of freedom, but we have turned to a substitute for the authentic.

Two important appetites—food and sex—are mentioned by Paul in 1 Corinthians 6:12–13. He said all things were allowable, but not necessarily profitable. God wants us to profit and abound! Paul went on to say all things were lawful, but he wouldn't be mastered by anything. Food is for the stomach. Also, the body is not for sexual immorality but for the Lord and the Lord is for the body.

Food, alcohol, and sexual excesses are illegitimate ways of trying to get intimacy or identity needs met. Filling up physical needs often masks the real needs of our souls. We try to push away our anxieties by numbing them but begin to become addicted while we are eating, drinking, or acting out our pain. But if we keep turning with these hungers to the Lord, he will meet us. He will help us unmask and heal what is hidden under our anxious excesses.

Our bodies, as well as our hearts, long for the Lord. "My heart and my flesh cry out for the living God" (Ps 84:2 NKJV). Every part of us can encounter God and receive his love. Often, physical healing comes into our bodies as we receive his love and presence into our souls.

Touch and Sexuality

We need the tactile because we thrive through touch. Touch has been called "the double sensation" because when we touch another we are also being touched. Touch helps infants grow, and touch deprivation may cause failure to thrive.

Psychologically, something happens when we touch; we are awakened and connected. The more whole we are, the more we can discern what is safe touch. And we ourselves are safe to others when we are fully at home within ourselves and can reach out with healthy touch. The more we are at home in ourselves, peacefully accepting ourselves, the more we embody Christ in the world as he expresses himself through us.

Our sexuality is a beautiful gift, part of our personhood, a dimension of our humanness created and blessed by God. Sexual intimacy with another is a deep connection with emotional and spiritual dimensions.

Broken sexuality can't be healed apart from our souls' involvement because sexual issues don't exist apart from our whole identity. Unrestrained sexual appetites which have opened the door to strongholds of lust often originated because of our deep needs for connection and the lack of bonding during early years. We are made for connection. Deprivation of it leaves us vulnerable to sexual sin.

In 1 Thessalonians 4:3–8 Paul tells each individual to learn how to "possess his own vessel in sanctification and honor" as part of spiritual formation (NASB). Interestingly, this is the same language Jesus uses in Luke 21:19 when he tells us to "possess" our souls. We may think of the body as less important, but how we use our bodies is especially important in our sanctification, so much so that Paul tells us to possess our bodies with honor. Paul also compares sexual sin to rejecting the Holy Spirit! And we can defraud others by misusing our bodies. We are to honor our bodies, honor others with our bodies, and honor the Spirit within us by governing our sexuality well (1 Cor 6:17–20). Sexuality is not just about our physical bodies, it is about our inner being.[85]

Maturity means making peace with our sexuality as we bring it to the altar, literally offering it to the Lord. We must be aware of its power toward others and within ourselves. Because we are not our own and have been bought with a price, whether married or single, we are called to purity. We direct this energy by self-regulation, so the river doesn't overflow its banks. When we use self-control we modify our responses rather than merely satisfying our own pleasure. Thus our redeemed sexuality expresses God's life in us and his love to the world.

Rest

We need sleep and we need rest, yet some of us are so restless we can't seem to quiet ourselves into a restful state. God has created us in his image, he has created us for rest, and he wants us to honor what he has created. If we are uneasy within our bodies and unable to rest, we might ask: "Body, what are you trying to say? What do you need?" Once you get the message and respond to it, the body can surrender to rest. Anxiety can lead to all

---

[85] West, *At the Heart of the Gospel*, 18.

kinds of sleep disorders, but scripture tells us that he wants to give sleep to his beloved (Ps 127:2). Our bodies may store and carry unacknowledged anger or anxiety, but once we acknowledge and deal with it, it will dissipate because the emotion is no longer suppressed and carried by the body.

Pause and Reflect

Is there an appetite—hunger, rest, touch, or another—that seems either undernourished or out of bounds in your soul? Write out how that distorted appetite is affecting your life and invite the Lord to give you insights into bringing it into appropriate bounds.

Dealing with Our Appetites

All appetites don't have to be satisfied all the time. In Philippians 4:12 Paul said he had learned the secret of contentment, how to be full and how to be hungry. Exercising contentment and self-control is something we need to learn as mature adults. He went on to say he could do all things through Christ who strengthened him. We can meet the demands of the bodily appetites with the affirmation that Christ lives in us, strengthening us. We are enabled to say no when necessary because of his presence.

The critical question is: What do we do with the force of our appetites since they have a crucial place in our being and are expressed by both the body and the soul?

Romans 6:6–14 is the key: "… Our old self was crucified with him, that our body of sin might be made powerless, that we should no longer be slaves to sin. … If we have died with Christ, we shall also live with him. … Even so consider yourselves to be dead to sin, but alive to God in Christ Jesus. Therefore, do not let sin reign in your mortal body to obey its lust … present yourselves to God … for you are under grace" (BSB).

We learn to consider ourselves dead to the pull and power of sin, at the same time presenting ourselves to God. This is our victory: the empowering of the Holy Spirit within us as we surrender to him. As we live out of this reality, he gives us the capacity to put our appetites to death in the right way (by self-control), enjoying them without being overcome by them.[86]

How do we develop self-control? It is a character quality as well as a fruit of the Spirit in Galatians 5:23, indicating the Lord's regulation and rule and influence within us. We call on him for help right at the place of greatest need. We learn to put sinful inclinations in check as we live more consistently by the Holy Spirit. Discipline does not come to us as a gift. Rather, it matures in us through choice.

Our bodies are the habitation of the Spirit, so we can either strive or we can yield to the Spirit who works self-control within us. Our spirit is willing though the flesh is weak (Mt 26:41; Mk 14:38), so we train our souls to yield to the Holy Spirit. Then self-control becomes a developed virtue. Thus, self-control is both a fruit of the Spirit and also a discipline being engraved in our character.

I know people, both men and women, who have been able to come free of addiction to pornography. By bringing their sin into the light, by confessing it to others, and by engaging consistently in small-group work, they received the prayer and support they needed to begin to overcome the habit. Then by leaning into the grace and empowering of the Holy Spirit, they developed more and more self-control and freedom from the pull and power of pornography. Every small success built their confidence and propelled them toward greater freedom and integrity.

More about Addiction

"We were created to be filled—humanity's miserable mystery is our insistence upon filling ourselves. We disconnect from the source of life."[87] The more we fill ourselves, the more addictions we can develop. St. Augustine called addiction "the cruel necessity." We need and seek, but it's never enough, like the fire of Proverbs 30 that will never be satisfied. Fires don't self-contain, and as long as there is air and fuel they burn and burn.

---

[86] Waterman, "Capacities and Motions of the Soul."
[87] Carla A. Waterman, *Songs of Assent* (Wheaton, IL: WaterManuscripts LLP, 2009), 36.

Addiction is that fire. C. S. Lewis called it "an ever-increasing craving for an ever-diminishing pleasure."[88]

Our patterns of addiction arise from our lusts, our long-practiced habits, our coping styles, and generational iniquity, then we can't deliver ourselves from them. We start to surrender to our false god and then we go under its power. Especially with the bodily appetites of sex and food, which are part of our essential design, we are prone to idolize their importance in our inner thoughts and emotional lives and in our outer lives and relationships. We develop rituals in our thoughts and our practices that enslave us, for "people are slaves to whatever has mastered them" (2 Pt 2:19 NIV).

Addiction is a complex issue that causes us much suffering and desperation while we are actually trying to avoid suffering. It's rooted in both the temptations we are continually yielding to and in unresolved pain and emptiness. We try to cope and escape because we didn't learn healthy strategies to relate to others and manage emotional distress.

Addicts are seduced into believing that the object or event will nurture them and meet their needs, but that is illusory. We are really looking for intimacy, belonging, meaning, joy, empowerment, vitality, acceptance, and worth.

The pathway of addiction starts when we feel emptiness, pain, shame, or fear and want to ease it. Then we start to get preoccupied with what soothes our anxieties and relieves or distracts us and we set up rituals in our pursuit of it. After we "act out," we feel shame, remorse, self-hatred, powerlessness, and hopelessness.

Long before getting completely out of control, a person has fought and lost many battles on the emotional level and feels hopeless. So, one of the great needs for addicts is hope. They often see no other options and they need hope to find practical options and to believe God's goodness and willingness to involve himself with them in the process. Our healing entails coming to the God of truth who has power to give us life and victory and render powerless that which has had power over us. We can begin with that hope.

If we allow our appetites to get out of bounds, addictions result. But when our appetites are in their place, a healthy intersect is created between

---

[88] C. S. Lewis, *The Screwtape Letters* (New York: HarperOne, 1942, 1996), 44.

the soul and the body. Because God's Spirit is within us, appetites no longer have the power to master us. Since we are alive to God, we can count ourselves dead to sin. The key is always his living presence. His Spirit, alive within us, enables and empowers our choices to welcome his reign and to exercise self-control. Every small step of obedience creates transformation within and points us to victory. Where we once surrendered our bodies to sin, we can now receive grace to master them.

Pause and Reflect

Is there any area in your life in which you can identify an addiction or a propensity to excess in a certain appetite? Write that out, being specific, noting when it started, and invite the Lord into that. Ask him to lead you into self-mastery.

Health and Freedom

God's design is that healthy patterns shape grooves into us during childhood, but for many of us that just didn't happen. Instead, unhealthy patterns were created, grooves were carved into thoughts, feelings, and behaviors creating channels for all future responses. They were initially reactions but they become choices when we are faced with what needs to change. Great victory will come when we dismantle addictive structures and habits, even relationships, and pay the price for new architecture. That new architecture should include people who can mentor us, and a community that nurtures transformation and understands the process of establishing new habits.

Habits have three components:

1. **The trigger or cue**, which is the pleasure stimulus, such as the delicious aroma of a cinnamon bun, which awakens desire.
2. **The action**, which is how I respond to that aroma, perhaps consuming that pastry.
3. **The reward**, which is dopamine being released into the body that makes me feel good for a bit, provides positive reinforcing feedback, and tells me to value what I've experienced.

Habits are hard to undo because they are firmly secured in the brain in a permanent circuit of memory that reinforces itself. Habits never go away, so we must develop better ones to supersede the old. This describes the exchanged life in Christ, reckoning ourselves dead to the old and alive to the new life-giving response. The reward is our freedom, and a great sense of joy from walking in the new way.

We need to have a vision for our own freedom. Our vision must be bigger than: *I just don't want to mess up*, because that is living defensively. We need to take responsibility to articulate each area, asking: What am I really hungry for? What do I need? How do I go about attaining it?

To grow in the Lord, we set small goals, and these goals work with our appetites. The banks of our river need to be strengthened with disciplined choices and wisdom in the areas of sexuality, food, drink, sleep, and exercise. We can also develop helpful spiritual disciplines around our appetites such as prayer, fasting, Sabbath rest, quietness and listening, journal writing, scripture meditation, practicing God's presence, community, and support groups. All of these contribute to reinforcing the new thoughts and behaviors with internal anchoring. This cultivates sturdy character.

Real freedom is energy brought under governance, so we need to design intentional ways of going forward. In the adult soul, our out-of-control appetites mask underlying pain and anxiety. To master these appetites—the struggle with life-besetting bad habits—we ask the Lord to help us deal with underlying patterns as we also choose to deal with appetites. We do both at the same time by refusing ourselves the "soothing" appetites and allowing the anxiety and pain to emerge. Then we work through those with the Lord and others.[89]

Conclusion: The Process of Gaining Freedom[90]

Freedom is offered to us and paid for in the cross, but there is a process involved in stepping into and walking out that freedom. In any addiction, we are in idolatry looking for someone or something else other than the

---

[89] Waterman, "Capacities and Motions of the Soul."

[90] Section summarized from video of Ruth Outram's "Addiction" presentation at Bethel School of Supernatural Ministry, Redding, CA, 2021.

Lord to give us fulfillment and comfort. When we continue to indulge in finding our satisfaction somewhere else, that object of satisfaction becomes compulsive and enslaving. Then shame begins to cover that object and we want to hide it in secrecy and isolation. The need is to find out what's really going on in our hearts and invite the Lord in right at this sore place.

It is at this point of need that we must know and encounter the love of God. We need to know that his love will not fail us, that he is for us and has purchased our victory. The freedom process has two elements:

1. God encountering us with his love so that we are enabled to walk into the process of change with hope. When God encounters us with his powerful loving presence, he meets us to forgive, heal, and deliver, making a new way possible. This often involves revealing and uprooting misbeliefs.
2. Our choosing and learning to walk in the freedom he has given us, growing in our understanding of our identity and empowerment. There is no substitute for steady growth in righteous habits.

If we only ever expect God-encounters, we may depend on the big moments and never learn to walk out the process of becoming victorious, powerful people, rewired in truth, full of the Spirit. We are to work with him in our formation, and we need to learn to use the tools he has given us. We must know the rituals we use and interrupt the cycle. We have to choose to break our secrecy and isolation and let people in, connecting to God and people in healthy ways instead of self-soothing.

We usually try to avoid or deny our difficult or painful emotions because we don't know what to do with them, so we soothe them the only way we know how. At first, we need self-awareness. What is going on inside of our hearts … what are we thinking and feeling and why? We articulate our thoughts and emotions to God and others and name our real needs. The Holy Spirit will always help us discover the answers to these questions if we ask him.

But we have to take the time to sit with the Lord and review: What happened today that prompted me to respond in such a way? What left me feeling like this? We can take time at the end of every day to review what happened and how we felt, and to write it out. This helps us connect our hearts and our actions. We begin to recognize our loneliness, isolation, rejection, our unmet needs, and the narratives we've been telling ourselves. Thoughts inform our emotions, so we can look at what we are thinking and believing.

Addiction is connected to a belief system filled with lies—lies of lack, rejection, hopelessness, incompetence, and all kinds of self-defeating untruths. This is the place where we invite the Lord in. We start becoming aware of what we are believing that's left an emptiness for God and others. Becoming aware of the ache, we can then invite the Lord into that, creating an occasion to encounter his love and truth. We come to know ourselves as his beloved—secure, known, accepted, deeply rooted, and one with him. Then we can make choices that lead to the life and freedom he has for us.

Pause and Reflect

To break the power of addiction, are you willing to face the pain? Are you willing to stay with the loneliness, anxiety, and any of the feelings that emerge, and bring them to his presence? (You may need to break your isolation and bring this pain to others as well.) This is such an important decision that will escalate our healing. This is the very thing we are avoiding but must face in our spiritual formation.

Prayer to Transform Appetites

First, thank God for your body. Release your body to him, taking quiet time before the Lord to give him each part of your body. Now move your body in some way so that you can feel the good of your body and praise him for the wonderful way you are made, and for the appetites that help you thrive.

Pray: Lord, where I have disparaged my body, living in some kind of shame or fear or hatred of it, I repent. I now give my body to you and choose to step out of those attitudes and live with gratefulness. Forgive me for any ways I have idolized or misused my body to gratify myself or manipulate and control others, whether food, sex, drink, overwork, or lack of rest. I repent of idolatry where I have let my appetites dominate.

Confess: What appetites are you having difficulty overcoming? What do you need to render powerless? Maybe a secret habit you have felt ashamed of? Confess that now and ask his grace to enter. He forgives you and is more than willing to engage you with his grace and help.

Name your secret habit to the Lord who already knows and receives you. Are you willing to face the pain of dying to any habit that has had dominion over you in the old way? Are you willing to stay with the loneliness, anxiety, the feelings that emerge, and bring them to his presence? Tell him this.

Pray: Lord, I repent of lies I have believed, especially that the objects of my appetite will give me the acceptance and love I want. I repent of shame and self-judgment. I set my heart and intention, by your empowering grace, to care for and honor my body. My appetites are gifts from you to help me live in healthy ways. Lord, I ask fresh grace for honoring my body. Grant me cleansing and the strengthening of my will so that I might face the inner wounds and pain that feed my appetites in wrong ways.

Release, Lord, your hope within me now, that real freedom is mine, that I can learn to walk in a new way, victorious. As you are compassionate toward me, let me have the same compassion toward myself as I learn to master over-indulged appetites. Bring transformation in the way I see and treat myself, in the way I respond to my appetites. Thank you that it's your love and presence that will do this. In Jesus's name.

Homework

Each morning in prayer, thank him for your body and yield your appetites to the Lord. If you have identified a habit that needs to change, enlist a partner or group that you can be accountable to as you face the process of change.

Recap

In our spiritual formation, we can make our bodies allies with our souls. When our appetites are in their place, a healthy intersect is created between the soul and the body and the energies of the body serve us rather than enslave us. Because our bodies are our domain, we take responsibility to govern and honor them. We can refuse to idolize the importance of our appetites in our inner thought/emotional lives and in our outer lives and relationships.

Now let's take a look at Part 3, Voices of Being and Formation, which include the sense of being, the masculine and feminine within our souls, and character formation.

PART III
VOICES OF BEING
AND FORMATION

9

SENSE OF BEING

Ronald Rolheiser writes that a healthy soul undertakes two things for us. "First, it must put some fire in our veins, keep us energized, vibrant, living with zest, and full of hope as we sense that life is, ultimately, beautiful and worth living. ... Second, a healthy soul has to keep us fixed together. It has to continually give us a sense of who we are, where we came from, where we are going, and what sense there is in all of this."[91]

What is a sense of being?

To have a healthy sense of being is to have the confident voice *I am.* To have a healthy sense of well-being is to have "personal vitality."[92] To lack this sense of well-being is to speak from an incomplete and insubstantial place. This deficiency affects the whole soul and can leave us feeling inner emptiness and lack of identity and trust.

To have a sense of being is to have a sense of fullness and richness as a person. It is the ability to genuinely say: *I am, and my personhood is good.* It involves the deep security of knowing we are, we have a solid existence, and that:

---

[91] Ronald Rolheiser, *The Holy Longing: The Search for a Christian Spirituality* (New York: Image Books, 1998, 1999, 2014), 14.
[92] Frank Lake, *Clinical Theology, Abridged* by Martin H. Yeomans (New York: Crossroad, 1987), 30.

- we have value, worth, and identity;
- it is well within us, and we can enjoy being vibrantly alive;
- we have the ability to trust and be connected with others;
- we belong, we have a place;
- we are competent and can handle life's difficulties; and
- there is no shame in being ourselves.

The one with a sense of well-being is free from undue fears and anxieties about the present or future. Even if you must wait, you know your needs will be met.

Our sense of being comes primarily from our early bonds with our mothers. The way mother handled our needs as a child shaped our lives, and what we learned in our relationship with our mothers deeply affects every area of our adult lives now.

What are moms supposed to give us by God's design? There are several specific areas foundational to our emotional and spiritual well-being. If we have lacked nurture in these areas, the Holy Spirit wants to meet us in healing.

1. **Safety and security**—This comes when mom is predictable, consistent, stable, and danger-free. Moms take care of the scary things at night, find you if you are lost, hold your hand as you cross the street, protect you from harm. Mom is to embody safety, and if she doesn't, you don't cultivate a sense of internal safety but instead develop anxiety.

2. **Nurture**—A mother's nurture from hugs, reassurance, eye contact, smiles, and affirmation brings replenishment, satisfaction, contentment, and a sense of well-being. When I was a child in the 1950s living in Scotland I awoke from a tonsillectomy longing for my mother. Hospitals were very different in that era, and I couldn't see her for another few days. I felt bereft of comfort and safety. In contrast, years later, sitting with one of my daughters as she awoke from a tonsillectomy, I was present, touching, soothing, telling her she would be fine. She received the needed comfort. Mothers' nurture replenishes our souls and we learn we can be soothed, safe, and calm instead of reactive.

3. **Basic trust**—When a mom responds to the child's needs with care, trust is established. Later this trust enables the child to reach out, to depend, to need without shame and fear, and to see others as the source of good things. In the reliance on this bond with mother, the child learns the beginnings of faith, trusting another who is faithful and good. Where this trust and attachment is disrupted, later adult relationships often are difficult.

4. **Belonging and invitation**—A sense of belonging anchors us and brings deep security. When you've been "invited" into relationship with mom through her love and care, it makes you feel wanted, which transfers into later feelings of worth and confidence in relationships. Being invited means mom has made room for you by arranging for you to have your own bed, a place at the table, a place to do homework, and a play place. It's what God does for us when he roots us into himself, establishing us deeply and firmly. Without a sense of belonging, we may develop a sense of abandonment, an orphan mentality.

5. **Someone to love**—Attachment and emotional development come not only from the mother's investment of love in the child, but also from the child's investment of love in the mother. This learned reciprocity is part of our necessary development, setting us up for healthy relationships in adulthood and discouraging the development of selfishness.

6. **Validation of gender and sexuality**—Moms validate their son's masculinity and sexuality by affirming their acceptability as a male and educating them about their development and about the opposite sex. They also communicate to their daughters that to be female is good and to be enjoyed and celebrated.

7. **Successful weaning**—A healthy mother attaches well and then helps her child leave well. As a child matures, the mother-child relationship should change as mom gradually lets go (but stays wisely available). In this way, we can more easily separate from mother's attachment and identity, becoming our own person. Psalm 131 expresses the inner peace of a child who has appropriately weaned from mother. We leave best when there is a healthy bond; otherwise, we experience a disordered detachment.

If we have these seven, we will develop a sense of well-being. Bonding to mother, being grounded in her love, is essential for our inner well-being. We learn how to regulate ourselves because her care has been internalized. This enables later healthy bonds with others as adults. The critical need of early development is a strong, nurturing bond between mother and child to set a foundation for adulthood. God designed us to need a sense of being and well-being from her. Our union with her gives us this. Without it, we can have such injury to our souls. When we are deeply attached to mother we feel: "I exist and it's good to be alive."

That sense of well-being is dependent also on the father's presence, guidance, and nurture, and to some degree, on life's circumstances. In fact, the child feels safest when both parents are present. The child feels: "I need both of you; I have both." When the husband loves his wife well she is able to nurture their child from a place of rest and solidity in her husband's embrace and covering. The child feels this safety.

Wholesome interactions with both parents set well-being into the child. Lake writes: "There are two vital needs of every child in these foundation years, which could be summed up as the face of the mother and the voice of the father; the smile of loving recognition and the word of guidance. We do not expect the child of three to have acquired much knowledge of revelation truth about the face of God and the Word of God from holy history. Yet it has acquired many permanently imprinted attitudes of expectancy or non-expectancy toward vital relationships."[93]

Pause and Reflect

As you read the description of sense of being, what was your first response in terms of recognizing your own sense of being and well-being?

Do you feel a lack of being or lack of well-being, any anxiety, or sense of deprivation?

Were you able to fully experience the seven areas of nurture foundational to well-being?

---

[93] Lake, *Clinical Theology, Abridged* 1987, 58.

Did you have nurture from both parents—the guiding voice of father and the loving face of mother?

How have you seen the Lord supply what you missed in these areas?

Over-Bonding with Mother

Psalm 22: 9–10 (NLT) declares: "You brought me safely from my mother's womb and led me to trust you at my mother's breast. ... You have been my God from the moment I was born." Because of this claim on our identity and destiny, Satan hates the relationship between mother and child and seeks to create enmity. He wants to wound the bond with our mom, causing it to be awry in some way, too thick or too thin.

In over-bonding, there is an unhealthy enmeshment with mother and a bond that is too thick. The mother may emotionally smother, be needy herself, be too controlling in some way, or even abusive. A smothering mother suffocates with too much involvement, a form of control over the child. Over-bonding is presented as love, but it demands control; it is evil wrapped in good. This mother can be manipulative, and this violates the child's personhood and boundaries. A child doesn't have a sense of his or her own well-being, just of mother's being and thus feels emotionally overwhelmed and confused.

This mother is unwilling to release her children and can create passive-aggressive sons. A mother who is too strict, including religious strictness, can crush spontaneous feelings and ideas. The real self of the child is stifled. This child may be raised not to express feelings, to deny his or her own inner life as bad or unimportant. As adults they then disqualify their own hearts because the authoritative parents were always right. And they may be entrapped in false guilt because they were trained to be responsible, often resulting in appeasement toward the adult parent rather than being able to stand as an adult and have their own feelings and choices.

In the orbit of a needy and hurting mother, the child feels the mother's chaos and the needs of the child are forgotten. This has been called "the tyranny of the weak," where the needy person holds the power. This can be an inversion of roles where the mother uses the child's protectiveness and loyalty to meet her own emotional needs. This is a form of emotional incest and violates boundaries. A child is never supposed to meet an adult's needs in this way! This scenario sets up children for later relational codependency, to meet the demanding needs of others and not recognize how to ask for and have their own needs met.

Fathers are to call out their children's identity, enjoy them, give them approval, champion them, and defend them. In the adolescent years father blesses the teen and guides him through emotional upheavals and reactions to mother. His saliency and firmness gives a son or daughter foundation and security in these years. He helps them manage their emotions, strengthens them, and calls them to maturity.

But when the father is absent from the home, or present but emotionally detached, the mother may try to fill in the gaps. When she tries to substitute as a father, that is a form of control. The son can be resentful and even become feminized and suffer from gender identity confusion.

An abusive mother sets up a thick bond from the emotional trauma, but the child is under-bonded in affirmation and nurture. The abusive mother is distant, disconnected, shaming, and critical. The child receives the message: "You aren't valuable, your needs won't be met, you'll be hurt." A mother's abuse may extend to sexual, physical, or spiritual mishandling and exploitation. The result can be that the child believes his or her role is to be the solution for the mom's abuse, thus giving a convoluted and false sense of importance or significance to the child, creating a trauma bond. The child feels responsible to be the container of mom's abuse so that the mother can function. Or the child keeps hoping for change, for the good things to come. Then, sadly, the child may keep bonding with others like mom later in life because it feels so normal and familiar.

All these scenarios create a sense of "not safe" within the child, whose feelings may include destructive patterns of fear, anger, shame, negative thinking, and even the hypervigilance of post-traumatic stress. They may not ever feel at "home" within, so they grow up anxious, without a sense of being and well-being.

Mothers like these create heart wounds that need deep healing and freedom. As adults, the sons and daughters first need to come out of any denial and recognize the destruction and their need for healing, naming the mistreatment and evil. They need to forgive their mothers and release any judgments against their mothers, while asking the Lord to heal their heart, and spiritually cut any inappropriate bond. If mother created an enmeshment, the adult child must come free of that.

Then, often the adult child needs to get help learning how to live with appropriate, honoring boundaries instead of appeasement. Adult children are in a position to honor (not obey) so they can love their mother while respectfully setting their own boundaries, living their own lives with integrity.

Pause and Reflect

As you have been reading this description of the over-bonding mother, can you identify any of these scenarios in your own life?

Specifically, how did you experience her control, neediness, manipulation, or enmeshment?

What do you need to forgive? Will you ask for the grace to do that now, and to cut the inappropriate bond with mother?

Deprivation and Separation

A bond with mother that is too thin and insubstantial leaves us empty. The bond feels tenuous, fragile, uncertain. It's like drinking from a very thin straw where you can't seem to draw up enough sustenance. When children's needs aren't met, they don't develop a secure bond and a secure sense of their own being. Emotional development is arrested. Neglect, a silent form of abuse, is often the issue here. The mother is under-involved and lacks attunement to the child's heart. When there is neglect, children do not feel secure in the love of the person who is their existence in the early years. The result is that a deep inner anxiety forms, an emptiness within, rather than a sense of well-being.[94]

Without a sense of being or well-being, there is a profound and lasting injury to the soul, perhaps even a sense of nothingness or nonbeing. Lake

---

[94] Frank Lake, *Clinical Theology,* (London: Darton, Longman and Todd, 1966), 1098.

wrote of the terrible consequences of deprivation when a baby does not have a mother's essential love.[95] He noted several causes for this:

1. If a child is rejected by the birth mother, the child feels this separation. If a baby is not able right at birth to bond with mom, he or she can come into the world feeling angry, rejected, needy, abandoned, and without a place in the world. Later the adult heart still feels orphaned, and so hungry and thirsty for love and acceptance.

2. Where there is prolonged separation from mother in the first two years of life, the child feels the deprivation as anxiety. This deprivation anxiety progresses from protest to despair, and then to detachment. First, when mom doesn't come, the baby protests with crying. A baby can't process the absence of mother, so after a prolonged separation, deep grieving begins. If mother still doesn't come, the baby loses hope because the little one can't sustain this separation anxiety. The baby withdraws in despair and may fail to thrive. Even when love at last comes, the baby may no longer be able to respond.[96]

This stage of detachment means the baby doesn't respond positively to mom once she comes. This stage can create a lot of sexual neuroses later on. The child has a gnawing sense of shame, emptiness, and deprivation—an elusive anxiety. Tension from the deprivation anxiety lodges in the baby's body, primarily in the genitals, then the little one clutches and rubs the genitals to relieve anxiety. This isn't driven by lust, it is driven by anxiety.[97] Later, as they develop, they may use a variety of anxiety relief supports, such as food, alcohol, or sex to assuage the anxiety. When deprivation anxiety is not healed, adults also feel it in the genital area and go into masturbation or sexual encounters. Tension collects from panic of separation or abandonment and the

---

[95] Lake, *Clinical Theology* (1966), 9–10.
[96] Mario Bergner, *Setting Love in Order* (Grand Rapids, MI: Hamewith Books, an imprint of Baker Book House Company, 1995), 80–83.
[97] Bergner, 82.

adult gives in to comfort. This anxiety may even develop into an inordinate attachment to objects in order to fill inner need.

3. The death of either parent during childhood results in deep deprivation. I once watched a PBS program about World War II, an interview with a man in his eighties. As he described the 1941 bombing of his neighborhood in Coventry, England, he remembered being an eight-year-old child holding his mother's hand, running for a shelter, when suddenly his mother was hit and died right beside him. Tears welled in his eyes as he told of this so many years later, still feeling the primal loss.

4. Other deprivations include the absence of father or mother from the home for extended periods; mental illness in either parent, but especially in mother; and emotionally wounded or stunted parents. When there are traumatic circumstances surrounding a childhood, now called "adverse childhood experiences," the child is deeply affected and may develop toxic stress response with physical symptoms.[98]

5. Where there is neglect, even unintentional, or emotional, sexual, or physical abuse, the child suffers from the lack of a secure and safe bond. Sometimes, more subtly—and due to her own deprivations—the mother's inability to give generously and kindly to her child creates a lack of connection and attunement to the child. And if there is actual violence, the parent figure, who should be the primary protector, becomes the child's enemy.

6. Other causes of this deprivation anxiety in a child can be shaming in the family, ignorance, poverty, sin within the family, illness in the child or parent, divorce, alcoholism, and drug use. Other conditions that may tend to leave children feeling in need are when parents are overworked, when children have to fend for themselves as latch-key kids, and when there are so many siblings that the child doesn't get enough attention.

---

[98] Nadine Burke Harris, *The Deepest Well* (New York: Houghton, Mifflin Harcourt, 2018), 54.

Loss of well-being is characterized by shame, inferiority, despair, a sense that there's not enough, an identification with emptiness and meaninglessness.[99] Deprivation can turn into fears, anxieties, dread, negative thought patterns, addictions, deep loneliness, feeling intellectually incompetent, depression, sensitivity to rejection, proneness to projecting issues onto others, deep suspicion and paranoia, a dark fantasy life, and a tendency toward introspection.

Those without a sense of well-being find it difficult to believe they can change because they feel no hope that the void could ever be filled. As a result, there can be lots of difficulty with adult relationships because love seems to have no staying power. Some seek to connect and attach homosexually, attempting to fill the deep need.

From these injuries, Lake writes of a loss of being, applying two images. He likens a loss of well-being to a tree in winter. Without leaves, it can look bleak and appear lifeless. But given the right conditions of spring rain and sunshine, its leaves gloriously burst out and the tree comes to life again. Leviticus 26:4 says that when God sends rain, the trees green and bear fruit again. As the Lord heals and brings our souls into a sense of well-being, healing the deprivations, everything is renewed and the life that has been dormant springs forth into vitality.

The second image reflects the loss of being itself as a "root out of dry ground" (Is 53:2). This tree is dried up, the stump is dead, and the earth around it is cracked. The dried remnant represents the dread and desolation of a loss of personal being. In this case, not only are the right conditions needed, but also a true miracle of God's life pouring in to impart being itself. To heal a lost sense of being will take this impartation of Christ's life, forming in us a bond with him where life and being flow in from him. Because Christ himself was thirsty and deprived on the cross, he becomes for us "the root out of dry ground" of Isaiah 53:2.[100] He alone can now wonderfully impart this life to our inner being.

---

[99] Lake, *Clinical* Theology (1966), 1098.

[100] Ibid., 1100.

Pause and Reflect

Did you identify yourself as a child in any of these scenarios or descriptions of the child without a secure bond?

If so, what happened and what emotions are you experiencing now?

Are you willing to invite the Lord into your situation?

Hope

To come free from a lifetime of deprivation we pray for an awareness of the fullness of Christ within, a true sense of being, where his life flows into us, bonding us to him, filling us. This means you come to know the one who created you in love and purpose. You learn that you are secure, you can put your full weight on him and feel you are on solid ground. He lives within and will never, ever leave you. Never could he forsake you (Dt 31:8).

"The filling of the human spirit with the life of God in obedient, loving fellowship with him is shown to be the only adequate answer to the predicament of emptiness and loss of well-being."[101] His life filling our very being!

Look how God bonds with us to give us being: "… that he would grant you, according to the riches of his glory, to be strengthened with power through his Spirit in your inner being [your true self]; so that Christ may dwell in your hearts through faith; and that you, being rooted and grounded in love, may be able to comprehend with all the saints what is the width and length and height and depth, and to know the love of Christ that surpasses knowledge, that you may be filled to all the fullness of God" (Eph 3:14–19 NASB). Pause and let that wash over you … the sense of your inner being filled with his life, the sense of being rooted in him.

Paul declared: "In him we live and move and have our being" (Acts 17:28 NIV). Then in 170 AD, Clement of Alexandria wrote: "For this he came down, for this he assumed human nature, for this he willingly endured the sufferings of man, that by being reduced to the measure of our weakness, he might raise us to the measure of his power. … Christ is

---

[101] Lake, *Clinical Theology* (1966), 1105.

the cause of our being as also of our well-being, and he has now himself appeared to mankind."[102]

The answer to our deprivations is to forgive mothers and fathers who were inadequate, receive Christ's healing for our wounds, and accept his indwelling life that gives us being. He shares our suffering in this and offers us his life. Then we practice his presence continually as our sense of being and well-being grows, rooted in his love. His resurrection life filling us makes this possible. We identify with his death and with his resurrection life. This is a process of lifelong healing that continues as we are grounded in his love.

In response to the prayer of faith, the Holy Spirit enters deep into the heart and mind, even the body, to create and restore a sense of being. Healing a sense of being and well-being may take place through a process with time and many prayers. We often need to grieve our childhood pain and loss that has been stored up, knowing he will receive our grief into his heart.

My experience with this is that over the years he has healed and deepened my sense of being and well-being. Even a few years ago I had a dream of my mother singing a lullaby over me, a vague and ancient memory within me of an exquisite Celtic tune I seemed to recognize. I saw her face and heard her voice, so present. I awoke with a beautiful comforting sense, thinking, "Oh, my mother really loved me." This was another part of God's lasting healing for me, settling into my heart again that I was deeply loved and kept.

Prayer

(Adapted from Leanne Payne, 1996, Pastoral Care Ministries)

Thank you, Lord, for showing me already where I need to forgive my parents or caregivers, especially my mother or stepmother for their lack toward me. You, Lord, know the pain and rejection. Jesus, you give me hope because you were rejected on my behalf.

---

[102] "The Characteristics of Alexandrian Theology," St Mark's Coptic Orthodox Church, accessed September 9, 2022, https://www.copticchurch.net/patrology/schoolofalex/I-Intro/chapter2.html.

Lord, you know where I have known great deprivation or emptiness. I acknowledge my pain from the neglectful, absent, or distant parent, or the enmeshment from a too-clingy mom, the mom who controlled, abused, or manipulated. I speak out my forgiveness as I name their sin.

I confess to you the different substitutes I have used: sex, alcohol, drugs, TV, food, relationships, or something so strange that I am ashamed, but it's given me a temporary relief. As I lay these out, Lord, I will to turn away from these so that I can feel the emptiness and cry out to you. I turn away from the poison cisterns and turn to you so that you can fill me with the true water.

Lord, where I have sinned in reaction by judging my mom or dad, forgive me as I forgive her or him. I ask that the dire effects of others' sin be bound and lifted from me. Thank you for dying for this. I lift to you the traumas I suffered through accidents or evil, sins against me, or the difficult circumstances that have robbed me. Come Lord, heal the deepest places of trauma, adversity, and lack. You know every moment of wounding. Where I have been diminished and minimized as a person, complete and fill me.

Untie me where I have been bound to my mother by crippling feelings of guilt, false responsibility, or demanded gratitude. Set me into my own adulthood. Lord, release me from any sense of needing to contain the diseased part of my mother or her emotions. Release me from needing to respond to mother's manipulations. Lord, cut the inappropriate bonds.

For Sense of Being

Lay your hand over your heart as you pray: Lord, you are the ground and source of my being. Now draw me right into the solidity of who you are. Come, Holy Spirit, and set into me a solid sense of self. I call on the name of Jesus, knowing in him I live and move and have my being. Fill me with your presence.

Awaken in me the capacity to connect, to bond fully with you and then with others. Give me a solid center from which to live. Come, Lord, and make solid that which is insubstantial or full of holes or cracks.

Engage your holy imagination with his work and see him come to make a solid place in you. See him fill the center of you, the deepest place of your being. See him create that solid core, strengthening you within.

For the Sense of Well-Being

See Jesus walking with you into that prison house of suffering where you have felt so alone. He comes into that isolated cell of confinement, taking your hand and walking with you out of loneliness, the pain of disconnection.

Where you felt such shame, even felt abandoned by God, he says: "You belong to me. Come to me. I lift your shame and replace it with my glory. You are my chosen, I delight in you, you are the joy of my heart. I am the center of all that you are, and all that you are is in me—your sense of being."

If you have felt like a dried and wintry tree, pray Psalm 1:3: Make me like a "tree planted by streams of water, which yields its fruit in season and whose leaf does not wither" (NIV). Breathe your life in me, Lord, so that I thrive. Let my true being be deeply rooted in you, with no fear of heat or drought, secure in you, an oak of righteousness, solid.

Homework

Daily invite him to fill you with the fullness of his life. As you do, with the eyes of your heart see him filling up your inner being, creating a solid inner center and a sense of well-being. Do this as often as you remember throughout the day, welcoming his presence.

Recap

To have a healthy sense of well-being is to have "personal vitality" and to be able to speak with a voice of confidence in our personhood. Our sense of being comes primarily from our early bond with our mother when we experience nurture, validation, and security. Where we have been deprived of this early bond, we can experience healing as the living Spirit fills our inner being with his life.

Now let's look at the masculine and feminine voices within our souls.

10

MASCULINE AND FEMININE

Professor Tom Howard said the distinction between the masculine and feminine is "the mightiest and most splendid of all distinctions in the universe … an imagery rich and hilarious with liberties and joys so far beyond gritty vocabulary."[103] It is mystery, deep mystery! Defining masculine and feminine is a bit like trying to define beauty: you have to see and experience something as beautiful because beauty is transcendent, mysterious, and captivating. Thus, the masculine and feminine must be experienced in order to be truly known.

The masculine and feminine within us are essential qualities that reflect God's true nature—his image.[104] They are capacities to be fully affirmed and cultivated. Male or female is our gender, but our souls have both masculine and feminine movement. Whether we are male or female, we have both. God created us in his image, and he holds both the masculine and feminine within himself.[105] His design is to release his image into humanity, in both male and female, revealing the masculine and feminine of himself.

Vital to our identity is our personhood in his image, with the strength and initiative of the masculine and the beauty and tenderness of the feminine. The relationship between the masculine and feminine within us reflects both our character and the character of God. However, what is

---

[103] Payne, quoting Jeffrey Satinover, *The Healing Presence*, 150.

[104] Payne, *Crisis in Masculinity*, 123.

[105] Eric Naus, "God's Feminine Attributes," *Crossroads* (blog), The Moody Church, July 5, 2011, https://www.moodychurch.org/gods-feminine-attributes/.

ours in creation may have been lost or disordered, and we can have severe gender confusion and serious confusion about our own masculine and feminine identity.

Two Attributes Within Our Souls

The voice of the masculine is *I initiate, act, and establish.* The voice of the feminine is *I receive, respond, and nourish.* Elisabeth Elliot wrote that the "distilled essence" of the masculine is initiation, while the essence of the feminine is response.[106] These two expressions—initiation and response—need to be joined and ordered within us, to dance together, both having place within our souls. But we can make the mistake of viewing these two aspects of our personhood as activities or roles. Our activities are not gender-specific, they are just activities such as leading, nurturing, golfing, cooking, making decisions, or creating. We have tended to assign certain roles to men and others to women. But what if we learned to be fully human, fully who we are in the Lord, and then allowed him to direct our activities, roles, interests, and desires? Under his grace we have freedom from rigid roles as he tells us who we are and what we are designed for, as he gives us dignity as persons to walk in the ways he has created for us.

We're comfortable thinking of God as masculine, as we should be. We pray: "Our Father." He fathers, acts, initiates, creates! We recognize that the true image of God as our Father is critical to our hearts. He blesses us, affirms us, guides us, corrects us, and gives us our identity in ways only a father can. He is full of authority, justice, courage, and leadership. We can trust this kind of father, one who always keeps his promises and has the power and wisdom to make wrong things right.

But he has true feminine characteristics as well. His first description of himself begins in Exodus 34:6–7 (ESV): "The LORD passed before him [Moses] and proclaimed, 'The LORD, the LORD, a God merciful and gracious, slow to anger, and abounding in steadfast love and faithfulness, keeping steadfast love for thousands, forgiving iniquity and transgression and sin.'" Until then, Israel had known him as "I Am," the God of power

---

[106] Elisabeth Elliot, *The Mark of a Man,* (Grand Rapids, MI: Revell, 1981), 55, 58.

who acted with authority and supremacy. But here we see traits typically assigned to the feminine, those of mercy and nurturing love.[107]

Since God holds within himself all masculine and feminine attributes, he wants to restore within each of us the polarity and the complementary of the true masculine and the true feminine. We need the divergence and the convergence of both for our souls to be whole. Sarah Bessey wrote: "God didn't set up a 'masculine' rule as his standard and plan for humanity. No, it was masculine and feminine together, bearing the image of God. New Testament scholar Daniel Kirk says, 'Only this kind of shared participation in representing God's reign to the world is capable of doing justice to the God whose image we bear.'"[108] In this shared participation he calls for masculine and feminine together to reflect his image.

We are to reflect both attributes of God—that is the fullness of our humanity. The masculine is holy strength, the feminine is holy beauty! The true masculine will look different in men than in women, and the true feminine in women will look different than in men. We are more fully man or woman when we are comfortable with the "opposite" attribute. A truly feminine woman is in touch with her masculine attributes. She needs the good of reason, the power to initiate, and the strength to speak in her true voice. The truly masculine man is in touch with his feminine attributes, the power to be responsive to God and to others. While the feminine takes in, the masculine takes hold of what's been taken in and acts upon it.

We can't possess the true masculine and the true feminine unless they are integrated within us, as both are necessary for the support of and the complement of the other. Otherwise, we lean too heavily into one and overbalance. So often we have been split off from one of the attributes. But our Redeemer has healing for us as we come to a greater understanding of the masculine and feminine so that we are integrated, balanced, and complete.

---

[107] Carla Waterman, "Capacities and Motions of the Soul."

[108] Sarah Bessey, *Jesus Feminist: An Invitation to Revisit the Bible's View of Women,* (New York: Howard Books, 2013), 79.

Pause and Reflect

Is the complementarity of the masculine and feminine within our souls a new idea to you? Until now, what have you been taught and shaped to believe about the masculine and feminine? Have you placed men and women in roles?

What would look different if the church were to understand and embrace the masculine and the feminine as God created them?

Have you considered God as having the fullness of both traits?

Now let's look at the two sets of attributes and how they move within our souls.

True Masculine (in both men and women)

The true masculine is the power to initiate, act, and launch out. Elements of the masculine include conceiving of and then giving shape to by defining, organizing, constructing, and forming—whether an idea, an organization, or an object—analyzing, and editing where necessary. The masculine organizes, leads, and exerts benevolent authority. It orients, directs, and takes responsibility and then is able to make tough choices and pierce through difficulties that may arise. When choices are made, there is an ability to stand firm in the choice, in convictions, and in truth. In fact, to move in the true masculine is wonderfully "to be empowered with Truth himself"[109] and thus able to honor the truth and walk in it despite opposition.

The true masculine sets boundaries and is able to determine what is beneficial and safe for others and for the self, confronting and protecting where necessary. Courage, justice, integrity, speaking the truth with conviction yet gentleness, are all necessary in this movement of the soul. Able to receive from others but resist manipulation from others, there is a strength of character in the masculine that enables stability.

This person, whether male or female, knows and acknowledges weaknesses, repenting where needed, and doesn't present a false front. In

---

[109] Payne, *Crisis in Masculinity*, 82.

short, the true masculine makes choices, even when difficult, and stands in them with courage and fortitude. We see all this in God himself, his divine "*power* to do good" in holiness and righteousness. The true masculine is awe-inspiring.[110]

The Masculine in a Man

"We understand much about a man when we are able to describe the role of masculinity in his life, in what way he embodies or fails to embody it, and how it relates to the feminine qualities in his character, whether he honors these or not, whether he accepts them in proper measure … whether he loves them or hates them, and whether masculine and feminine within him serve each other or are at war."[111] A man's character is reflected in his ability to hold both the masculine and feminine within his soul in a way that honors both. A godly man gives dignity and honor to women. Pope John Paul II wrote that the dignity of every woman is the responsibility, the duty, of every man.[112]

Men are in a unique position to invite women to share headship, to make collaborative decisions. We see this in 1 Peter 3:7 where husbands are exhorted to be considerate toward their wives, showing them honor as joint-heirs of the grace of life in shared participation. When a man honors women, he honors the true feminine and is thereby strengthened in the grace of the feminine.

In a healthy man, the true masculine attracts women who are healthy, and this man richly blesses and receives the feminine. He isn't macho and controlling in his approach, but able to be gentle in his firmness. He is centered not in what he does but who he is. He embraces his sexuality responsibly and is able to respond and be alive to his wife. Men are strengthened in their true masculine as they receive the feminine power to respond and be penetrated with the presence, wisdom, and fear of the

---

[110] Ibid., 8.
[111] Ibid., 124.
[112] Christopher West, *Theology of the Body Explained*, 365.

Lord. A man reflects sturdy self-acceptance because he knows that he's accepted by Father God.[113]

A truly masculine man reflects and deposits order, truth, and strength. He uses his God-given authority well and brings protection and life to others by it. "A man reflects God by remembering what is important and moving into a disordered situation with the strength to make an important difference. A masculine man never forgets that he bears God's image, that nothing matters more than bringing Christ's kingdom to earth by crossing the bridge to strongly enter the lives of others with divine weight."[114]

Masculine qualities are more of the doing and acting, often more cognitive, logical, and scientific. If a man doesn't have the complementary of the true feminine within his soul, the false masculine can take over. Both capacities must operate in tandem and in balance or something is amiss in the soul.

False Masculine in a Man

What characterizes the false masculine in a man is based in insecurity instead of self-acceptance, in feeling unaffirmed in his true masculine, and in lacking connectivity with God and others. "Men who are unable to fully accept themselves lose to one degree or another the power to act as father, husband, leader. … They remain immature … unable creatively to initiate the changes needed to lift themselves and their families out of the inevitable quagmires of life."[115] This man uses activism and roles to define himself because he lacks a true, solid center. He is busy with work or other pursuits, but at a cost to his soul and his own spiritual strength.[116] He is able to *do*, but not to *be* because he does not have internal affirmation.

The man in this position gets his identity through his roles in work, sports, education, economic conquest, and sexual prowess. This performance-based identity echoes God's response to Adam's sin: the requirement that Adam live by the sweat of hard work in order to be

---

[113] Walter Trobisch, *The Complete Works of Walter Trobisch* (Downers Grove, IL: InterVarsity Press, 1987), 603–643.

[114] Larry Crabb, *Fully Alive,* (Grand Rapids, MI: Baker Books, 2013), 67.

[115] Payne, *Crisis in Masculinity*, 11.

[116] Dan Allender, *Leading with a Limp* (Colorado Springs, CO: WaterBrook Press, 2006), 130.

productive (Gn 3:19). With the fall, work potentially became identity itself instead of being an expression of identity. In this twisted expression of identity, often there is a drive for money, position, and success to gain worth. The raw "drive toward power," a perversion of the true masculine, is dangerous.[117] All the driven activity creates emotional numbness. This cuts a man off from the good of the feminine because he feels threatened by it. He is split off from his intuitive heart so he can't really experience God and others in healthy ways. He flees from feelings and intuition and hides from relationships.

A man stuck in the false masculine can be overly objective, suppressing emotion, and dependent on analysis only. This makes him unapproachable, which is his defense to being tender and vulnerable. He attempts to control by domination, perpetrating real pain on others in his narcissistic leadership. He may intimidate or manipulate, forcing others to meet his counterfeit expectations. When a man does not step into his true authority, he will substitute control.

If a man refuses to let true feminine qualities in, he will demand only the logical and provable. This insulates him from the intuitive heart and from relationship with others. He needs the true feminine for worship and responsiveness to God, for hearing the Spirit, which is so central to our Christian lives. The false masculine keeps a man in activism, driving for power, but it hides the deep yearning to be quiet in the Lord's presence, to express his heart, to really listen.

A man can be healed in his masculinity by taking in the love and nurture of God, hearing God's voice define him and give him identity. "Men are only healed in their true masculine—the power to initiate and to do the full will of God—as they are strengthened in their bridal identity. This is the power to respond and be penetrated, through and through, with the fear of the Lord—the fear of a masculine that is so powerful that we are all feminine in relation to it."[118]

---

[117] Payne, 88.

[118] Payne, *Listening Prayer*, 85.

True Feminine (in both men and women)

The true feminine is of the heart, the being, the creative-intuitive dimensions of our souls. The true feminine is the capacity to be fully alive and responsive. It is relational with all that is responsive to God, others, and nature. There is true receptivity in the feminine motion of the soul. Wonderfully, as our responsiveness to God grows, we are capable of receiving even more. We see this in Luke 1:38 (NKJV) when Mary responds to the angel: "Let it be according to your word" and receives the seed of God. We receive into the womb of our spirits more of God, more of the true and beautiful as we respond and say yes to him.

Likewise, Mary of Bethany sat at the Lord's feet, captive to his words, receiving. Her choice is a picture of the feminine motion of the soul, able to listen, to wait, and to surrender in humility. The true feminine is also able to nurture what is received, to bring to birth, and then to protect the emerging young. The inclination of the feminine is to respond to those who are weak. The true feminine is also sensitive to danger, is discerning, and senses deeply with perception and a quiet, internal knowing at a deep, intuitive level.

In the true feminine is surrender, that ability to yield and submit appropriately to what is true and good. And there is the tenderness of vulnerability, but deep strength can rise from this tenderness. Within the true feminine is also the ability to respond and to be fully alive sexually.

True Feminine in a Woman

Larry Crabb wrote: "A woman is feminine when she relates in a way that invites others to see something about God that is irresistibly attractive, something about the relational nature of God that she was created to enjoy and reveal. She invites movement toward her and embraces the movement she receives. She invites, rather than demands or controls."[119] She civilizes and softens the masculine in a man, like the true masculine in a man strengthens the feminine in her. When she receives and honors the true masculine within men, she is strengthened in that grace. The true feminine

---

[119] Crabb, *Fully Alive,* 41.

always needs to be wedded to and balanced by the true masculine. If not, the false feminine abounds.

False Feminine

The false feminine, like the false masculine, is characterized by insecurity, and especially by passivity. Passivity may turn into sloth, a reluctance to show up in one's life with all of one's passion and presence available. This often leads to depression because there is not a real person living from her own being. In the false feminine, a person is able to "be" in a passive way, but not able to move forward and initiate. Passivity is not receptivity; a person is simply being acted upon. Overly submissive compliance means someone else is making your decisions. You have lost your own true voice, given up making your own decisions and exercising the good of your reason; you have given up your real self. This is never what God intends.[120]

The false feminine is characterized by the underdeveloped masculine. A person may have meaning and being, can sense and intuit, but be unable to give form, substance, and direction to what is sensed. They "feel" but don't know what to do with it, how to shape it and take it further into action. They have difficulty in editing, in giving order and direction to thoughts and feelings. There is lack of clarity, lack of vision; choices are based mostly on feelings without the good of reason. The false feminine can also develop into hyper-spirituality.

The false feminine uses roles and activities as a substitute for the self. It is also characterized by codependency, orbiting around others with their feelings, neediness, darkness, and demands. (Of course, men can fall into these patterns as well.) We can bend into another person's neediness or pain to coddle them instead of loving them and speaking the truth with integrity. The false feminine is easily deceived or manipulated into meeting the counterfeit expectations of others. But it can also seduce and manipulate, which is a perversion of the true feminine power of appeal.[121]

---

[120] Leanne Payne, Lecture on Listening Prayer at School of Pastoral Care Ministries, July 1996, Wheaton, IL.
[121] Waterman, "Capacities and Motions of the Soul."

Women in the False Feminine

Women suffer deeply in broken relationships where there is a disconnection of love and closeness. This is echoed in Genesis 3:16 where we see the unredeemed woman bent toward her husband and in pain bearing children.

The false feminine can emerge out of a deep desire for change in another person's life. We can so passionately want what we think is right for somebody else that our own intense desires become the lens through which we see them. We don't see them objectively. For instance, normal human desires in marriage may get hyper-focused on the husband who isn't reciprocating. Our needs then permeate every way we see our husbands; we reinterpret everything they do through our grid of what we want to happen. It isn't about what the actual person is doing, it's about our grid.

Christian women may want their husbands to become more receptive, so they try to find a way to get their husbands to become more open, more emotionally and spiritually intimate. This is the false feminine trying to engineer another person and make them into the image we think we must have for our happiness. This manipulation to force another to meet our expectations trespasses on their will. Only the Lord can work good things in another. We have to continue to let them go, surrendering passive and active control, instead of "crawling into their internal space."[122]

If I as a woman refuse to let both feminine and masculine traits develop well and in balance, then I'll become overly dependent, passive, compliant, and controlled. Or I will become controlling. Or if I have been damaged as a woman and out of that pain and anger I take on a masculine demeanor for self-protection, that is the false feminine as well.

Pause and Reflect

In what ways do you recognize the false feminine and/or the false masculine within your soul?

Have you as a man ignored or devalued the true feminine graces? Have you as a woman feared or devalued true masculine qualities?

---

[122] Ibid.

Would you invite the Lord into that now, to begin to show you the truth and bring healing?

Enmity

The false masculine and false feminine are at war! This power struggle is based in distortion and lies. Instead of serving and honoring one another as men and women, there is enmity. When the true masculine is feared or hated that is called misandry and is usually a response to pain perpetrated by men. When the true feminine is feared or hated that is called misogyny. Those threatened by the true feminine will diminish, fear, or try to destroy it in others. Misogyny splits us off from the intuitive faculty, the ability to really experience God and others. Men and women in misogyny run from the true feminine—from women, from feelings, and from intuition. It often looks like devaluing, dismissing, and disrespecting women by making the feminine less valuable than the masculine. When Christian leaders, sometimes blind to their own misogyny, diminish the feminine, women learn to put to death the masculine, that ability to shape and initiate within themselves. They never have had permission to fully and truly be. But God gives you that permission today. He calls it forth! Hear him today.

For both men and women, discomfort with the true masculine or true feminine causes a lapse into the false. A truly masculine man is in touch with feminine attributes of intuition, wisdom, and nurture as he leads and initiates. A truly feminine woman is in touch with masculine attributes and can initiate and lead without damaging, controlling, and trespassing the boundaries of others.

Healing is about restoring the polarity and complementarity of the masculine and feminine. True masculinity is always wedded to true femininity. The feminine in us takes in the word and receives it, then the masculine acts upon it and builds. The false feminine is only capable of being acted upon. The false masculine plunges into building without first waiting and receiving the word. But the true feminine and masculine operating in tandem produce wonderful results.

Redemption

The role of prophet epitomizes both true masculine and true feminine. First, the prophet has to receive the word of the Lord, a receptive, feminine movement of the soul. Then with the true masculine the prophet speaks forth the word courageously, persists in what has been said, and acts to call people to righteousness. Jeremiah was such a prophet and scripture says God's words in Jeremiah's mouth were fire. He wrote (15:16 NIV): "When your words came, I ate them; they were my joy and my heart's delight … ." That's the feminine receptivity. Then, in the masculine voice, he spoke those words out to Israel, often declaring: "Woe to you! Repent!"

Jeremiah spoke, then courageously stood in what he spoke without wavering, even facing death (26:15). Although speaking with such fire stirred up the people and brought down curses, reproach, and derision on him (Jer 15:10, 20:8), he knew the Lord was with him like a dread champion. That's the true masculine! Yet Jeremiah also voiced the Lord's nurturing redemption: "I have loved you with an everlasting love; Therefore I have drawn you with lovingkindness. Again I will build you and you will be rebuilt" (31:3–4 NASB).

David is another example of both expressions. In 1 Chronicles 28:19 (NET), David, the battle-weary warrior who still had a heart to build God a house, wrote: "All this I put in writing as the Lord directed me and gave me insight regarding the details of the blueprints." (That's the feminine receiving, becoming pregnant by the Spirit.) Then David turns and in the true masculine gives a clear exhortation to Solomon to get on with it. "Be strong and courageous and act; and do not fear nor be dismayed, the Lord God, my God, is with you. He will not fail nor forsake you until all the work for the house of the Lord is finished" (28:20 NASB). David, in a display of the masculine executing what was received, had stockpiled materials and prepared a team of skilled people to help Solomon.

Deborah also had both masculine and feminine in balance. She was a prophet and judge who was leading Israel (Jgs 4:4ff) when Barak asked her to go with him into battle. She was reluctant but once there she directed him to proceed into battle, promising the Lord would give him complete deliverance. Later she composed a song about arising (5:7) as a mother in

Israel. She demonstrated both the feminine mothering and the decisive, directing masculine movements of the soul.

A whole, real woman is in awe of the true masculine in a man, his strength and protectiveness, his power. A real man is moved by the beauty, tenderness, and strength of the true feminine operating through a woman. The true masculine is able to bless the true feminine and vice versa.

We need balance—a woman needs the true masculine within to form and shape her meaning, gifting, and intuition, and to be released to be who she really is. When she receives and honors the true masculine within men, she is strengthened in the grace of the masculine. A man needs to bring the drive for power under submission to Christ—he needs that leadership quality to be softened by tenderness toward others. When he honors women, he honors the true feminine and is thereby strengthened in the grace of the feminine. We support, affirm, nurture, and heal one another in this way.[123]

Each needs to be informed and balanced by the other. Both men and women can be nurturing, responsive, and also able to be and speak truth, to initiate, build, and shape. The masculine and feminine complete each other. The fullness of the church depends on this important interplay, as well as the honor of each toward the other. When men and women stand up with both the power to act and lead and the power to love and nurture, there is no stopping the church!

Pause and Reflect

Would you ask the Lord for a fresh vision for his body, the church, so that men and women move together in leading and loving and releasing God's presence?

---

[123] Payne, *Crisis in Masculinity*, 132.

Prayer for Strengthening and Ordering of True Masculine /Feminine

God loves how he made you! Repent now of any self-hatred or rebellion toward being the gender that you are, for parts of your body or yourself that you haven't liked. Naming the wound, forgive any who wounded you in your identity as male or female.

He loves how he made you! God has made you a man or a woman. Now receive his affirmation of you as a man or a woman.

For women: Lord, fill me with both true feminine and true masculine as I receive from you. Balance within my soul the feminine/masculine movements.

For men: Lord, fill me with both true masculine and true feminine as I receive from you. Balance within my soul the masculine/feminine movements.

Pause now and let him minister to your soul.

For those stuck in the false masculine, in the bent to power and control: Lord, I humble myself and repent of my drive toward power and control and ask you to release and restore only true power with gentleness, honor, and benevolence. Work this in me. Lord, heal now and release in me the true relational-intuitive mind.

For those stuck in the false feminine: Lord, I repent of passivity, codependency, manipulation, and control. I repent of any idolatry toward any other person. Lord, release the false and restore beauty and strength in me.

For those who feel they have had to be strong all their life and have lost the power to nurture, have lost the true feminine within: Lord, heal and restore the true feminine within me. Bring me to the truth of who I am and release the need to always be strong.

For those who can only respond to others and cannot make decisions and find their own voice, who have lost the true masculine: Lord, heal and balance the true masculine within me. Grant me the ability to initiate, to move forward, to analyze and act. Heal any confusion of gender, of who and what I am. Resurrect in me true gender identity. Awaken within me what has been covered and asleep. Call to life within me the true masculine/feminine and set them in order, in balance, in union.

For women who need more of the true masculine ability to shape and build: Lord, impart the true masculine so that authority, initiation, decision-making, and truth come more strongly into my soul.

For men who need more of the feminine ability to respond and receive: Heal this, Lord, so I won't fear tenderness and vulnerability. I repent of any fear or hatred of the true feminine. Bring the masculine and feminine into order within my soul, Healer. Thank you for the power of the cross to set all things in order.

Homework

If you have been able to identify an area where you are weak in the true masculine or true feminine, write this out in your spiritual journal and make it a daily prayer for the next month. Ask the Lord to strengthen this area, to pour his life in and bring healing.

Recap

The masculine and feminine qualities within the soul are essential, mysterious, and vital to our personal identity. As a revelation of God's true character, they reflect the integration of both initiation and response. They need to be understood, affirmed, balanced, and cultivated in their true expressions within our souls.

Now let's look at the last voice of formation, that of character.

11

CHARACTER

We experience real transformation as we become mature and complete in Christ. As we experience continued growth and transformation throughout our lifetimes, Jesus is taking over increasingly more ground in our souls—revealing, conquering, and redeeming the depths and intricacies of our souls. When the Lord is working within, he re-creates every capacity of our souls, omitting nothing, so that we become his masterpieces. Our collaboration in this process is essential. So, we pray that he will give us a deep hunger to want to grow more, knowing more of him within our souls.

Pause and Reflect

Let's stop and ask for that. Lord Jesus, take over ever more of my soul, healing, cleansing, and enlivening every part of me. Burn away the old and set me ablaze with you. Lord Jesus Christ, speak to my heart, change my life, and make me whole.

Voice of Our Character

Inner character consists of our attitudes and inclinations—inherent, deeply rooted qualities of our minds and natures. These temperaments are energies of the heart that have settled into patterns. Character can be considered an assembly of our desires, emotions, and dispositions which have become habituated within us.[124]

The healthy inner voice of our character says, *I form, mature, deepen, and move toward wholeness and integrity.* The false voice can be a voice of stagnation and unwillingness to grow that says, *I'm hopeless and powerless.* Or it can be a voice that says, *I will grow in my own self-deceived, self-oriented way and run after self-fulfillment.*

Our underlying tendencies toward settled moods are those inner attitudes that direct our thinking, emotions, desires, and responses. These patterns have developed over years, etched within, often without our even realizing they have become our habitual tendencies. For instance, we become a person who is patient or bitter, sensitive or callous, deceitful or honest, pure or carnal. These tendencies may be very natural to us, but God wants to reorder our disordered tendencies. God knows our inmost passions and knows just how to get to the deep places to transform our temperaments, to make us more like him.[125]

An example of this is a person who has generational anger. Born into a family who expressed unhealthy anger, a bitter disposition, and even explosive rage, they learned to hold resentment and express emotions in these ways. Perhaps no healthy examples were modeled. However, as the Lord begins to highlight the need for transformation, grace will be available to repent and to learn new ways.

Whether instinctive or learned, responses in our early years formed habits, which in turn formed our character. As adults, we can see our need to form new virtues that strengthen us within and give us constancy and integrity. By faith, when we continue to walk in the Spirit, renewing our hearts and minds with his word, we meet life's challenges and develop new habits of response, engraving them within our souls. In this way our virtues become "embodied in habits."[126] To pursue real transformation, we partner with God and take in the words that heal, order, correct, give new life, and establish new patterns.

---

[124] Anthony T. Kronman, *The Lost Lawyer: Failing Ideals of the Legal Profession* (Cambridge, MA: Harvard University Press, 1993), 16.

[125] Waterman, lecture series.

[126] C. S. Lewis, *The Screwtape Letters* (New York: HarperOne, 1942, 1996), 28.

Merriam-Webster traces the word *character* to the Greek word *charassein,* which means "to sharpen, cut in furrows, or engrave." The corresponding Greek noun *charkter* indicates a distinctive quality. So, our character is what has been chiseled into us and given us distinctive qualities, often a painful process. A change in character is not something that just happens to us. "The Spirit's conquest of our fleshly nature is not necessarily automatic. We have a choice in the matter."[127]

Not every Christian is fully alive in the vitality of the freedom promised us in Christ. Many, by choice and habit, are still enslaved. We can read scriptures, the promises of freedom and fruitfulness, and realize we are not experiencing all of this yet. We feel constricted, compelled by old tendencies. Here is where his grace and our moral effort have to come together. By choice, we give everything we have, and God pours in everything we need to obey. As we repeatedly say yes to his enlivening Spirit we are changed and new character is etched within.

We see this principle in Philippians 2:12–13 (PHILLIPS): Continue " ... to work out the salvation that God has given you with a proper sense of awe and responsibility. For it is God who is at work within you, giving you the will and the power to achieve his purpose." His enabling grace is always ours as we set our hearts and minds toward him in loving obedience, partnering with him to look like Jesus. Where we see brokenness in any area, we can be confident that grace will abound even more through the Lord Jesus Christ (Rom 6:20–21).

Character qualities in us comprise our inclinations and nature, whether of the Spirit or of our flesh. In scripture, godly qualities are expressed as the fruit of the Spirit: love, joy, peace, patience, kindness, goodness, faithfulness, gentleness, and self-mastery (Gal 5:22–23). Immediately before this list we see the dispositions or passions that are of the flesh. Quite a contrast! God is always drawing us to the fruit of the Spirit. As the Holy Spirit works within us and we cooperate, each quality begins to become more settled, maturing into virtue. The fruit of the Spirit takes shape within us little by little, building and growing. Every time we yield in obedience, he is able to build in us more of his holy character. We find more joy, more love, more of each virtue. These virtues are deep and noble inner qualities that strengthen us to stand well and to be steadfast in our

---

[127] Paul Billheimer, *Destined for the Cross* (Wheaton, IL: Tyndale House Publishers, 1982), 24.

expressions of the nature of Jesus. They help provide solid inner structure to our souls, a necessary foundation to live out our Christian lives and to express our gifts and callings.

The Spirit has taken up residence within us and when we abide in him, we find intimate communion with him. That intimacy begins to change our temperaments and establish our character. We all carry giftings and anointings and he cares about how we carry these because he has productive assignments for us. But our giftedness is not a measure of character. Our character should be able to carry the weight of our assignments so that we are truly fruitful. Our gifts, empowered by the Spirit, should reflect the presence of his nature within us and bring glory to him. When Paul wrote to Titus (2:10–14 NET), he said that God has come "to purify a people who are truly his, who are eager to do good," which will "… bring credit to the teaching of God our Savior in everything."

But we may counteract the blessing of the gifts if our character is flawed. For instance, I may desire to teach good things and help people grow in maturity. But if I am impatient with people when growth is slow, if I have perfectionistic or egocentric expectations, if I try to control others, I will be disqualified from really helping people and instead cause wounding. The expression of our gifts, united with his character, brings glory to his name and fruitful ministry to his people.

The Exchange

In contrast to the fruit of the Spirit, Galatians 5 also lists ungodly passions such as drunkenness, sexual immoralities, depravity, idolatry, strife, bitterness, malice, jealousy, anger, selfish ambition, and slander. These impulses and desires of the flesh are in direct opposition to the Spirit. These are "dispositions which must be continually yielded to the cross and death if we are to live triumphant and victorious lives."[128]

What do we do about this? The same passage gives us the answer: "And those who belong to Christ Jesus have crucified the flesh with its passions and desires" (Gal 5:24 ESV). This is echoed in Romans 6:3–14 (NIV), where Paul writes of being baptized into Christ's death, buried with Him,

---

[128] Billheimer, 23.

in order to walk in a new way. We are crucified with him that the old self might be "done away with," literally rendered powerless.

Having died with Christ, rendering the old self powerless and unable to dominate, we now live by the power of Christ. When Paul writes of putting to death the old self, he's referring to uncontrolled appetites and ungodly passions, not to our minds, wills, imaginations, and other capacities of our souls. It is these ungodly passions, along with uncontrolled bodily appetites, which discolor and pollute everything, keeping lies in place, literally bringing rottenness to our bones.

Roy Hession, in *The Calvary Road* wrote:

> It is always self who gets irritable and envious and resentful and critical and worried. It is self who is hard and unyielding in its attitudes to others. It is self who is shy and self-conscious and reserved. As long as self is in control, God can do little with us, for the fruit of the Spirit with which God longs to fill us is the complete antithesis of the hard, unbroken spirit within us and presupposes that self has been crucified.[129] ... The willingness of Jesus to be broken for us is the all-compelling motive in our being broken too.[130] ... Dying to self is not a thing we do once for all, ... it will be a constant dying, for only so can the Lord Jesus be revealed constantly through us. All day long the choice will be before us in a thousand ways ... so that there is yet a deeper channel in us for the life of Christ.[131]

To understand and practice this daily death to self is critical to maturity. We die to the old tendencies and ways and put on the new. Colossians 3:3, 10 (NIV) says: "For you died, and your life is now hidden with Christ in God. ... Put to death, therefore, whatever belongs to your earthly nature. ... Put on the new self ... ." Because we have a new life with Christ, hidden in him, we now have the capacity to put on his life

---

[129] Roy Hession, *The Calvary Road* (Fort Washington, PA: Christian Literature Crusade, 1950), 22.

[130] Hession, 23.

[131] Hession, 25.

and walk in a new way. Romans 7:5–6 (NIV) tells us that "… by dying to what once bound us" we can now "serve in the new way of the Spirit," the Spirit of life in Christ.

How is this done? It is a death by exchange with life, one thing substituted for another. We see an example of this in Lewis's *The Great Divorce,* where a man has a red lizard of lust on his shoulder whispering in his ear, whipping him with its tail.[132] A flaming Angel asks the man if he'd like him to quiet the lizard for him. The man agrees, but when the Angel wants to kill it, the man says: "You didn't say anything about *killing* him at first. I hardly meant to bother you with anything so drastic as that. … Look! It's gone to sleep of its own accord. I'm sure it'll be all right now. … I'm sure I shall be able to keep it in order now. I think the gradual process would be far better than killing it."[133] The man wanted to manage on his own, apart from death to self.

The man keeps wavering while the Angel keeps asking permission to kill it. The Angel won't bargain, won't change the terms of freedom, yet can't kill it without the man's permission. There is only the one way, and the man feels the heat, the discomfort of the burning Angel's nearness. The man, miserable, finally decides the death would be preferable than having to live with that creature. So, the flaming Angel gets a burning grip on the creature and the man screams in agony. The man, who had been so insubstantial, turns into an immense, solid man, full of light and joy. The lizard has been transformed into a great stallion, beautiful and powerful, able to carry the man.

This is the amazing strength of self-mastery. Our willingness to die to the old passions opens the door for the Spirit to establish the new. It's the same energy, but it's exchanged and transformed. The energy of sexuality, transformed and brought into mastery, became the fire and power carrying the man. What has to be reckoned with is our need to die to the old and our permission for it to be gone in whatever form it has taken. In that exchange, we are overcome by his new life so that we may truly become ourselves. Death is the only way, and it may burn and cost us, but it won't kill us. It will be our salvation.[134]

---

[132] Lewis, *The Great Divorce* (New York: Collier Books, 1946), 98–105.
[133] Lewis, 99.
[134] Waterman, lecture.

How we respond to pressure, stress, temptation, and trials has a great deal to do with how our character develops. If we choose to remain in joy during trials when our faith is tested, then steadfastness will develop (Jas 1:2–4), a quality of completeness and maturity of character. As our faith stands the test of distressing pressures, what results is proven character that produces praise and glory and honor to the one who is worthy (1 Pet 1:6–7). Trials and suffering ground us in him more deeply and develop godly character with channels where his life can flow.

God isn't repairing the old self; he's inviting it to die and be replaced with his life. Quite an exchange! Transformation of soul has to do with this death-to-self process. It is a choice to be free rather than just to be safe. To stay in self-protective safety is to stay bound.

The indwelling of the Holy Spirit is fundamental to our transformation. He guides us through the process of growth to renew and re-form every capacity of our souls. Our union with Christ makes growth possible. It is in our surrender, not our striving, that we see real change. Striving in our own strength will bring discouragement if we fail to see the broken places change. But the possibility of healing exists because Jesus really lives within us and has created a whole place within us. Sarah Colyn writes of this: "The erring and hopeless voices of world, flesh, and devil would tell you that you are your wounds, that you are most truly named by the damaged places in your soul. Answer those voices with confidence, testifying that you have received the most valuable privilege that exists: a place of wholeness already established inside your own being. … This is an amazing, invisible reality, and one that your soul needs to ponder, imagine, profess, and own."[135] Christ lives within us and is making us whole.

Pause and Reflect

Stop and put your hand over your heart and thank him that he lives within you, that he has created a whole place already inside of you. Take that in. What incredible grace!

---

[135] Sarah Colyn, "Meditations on Wholeness in Christ," Ministries of Pastoral Care newsletter, July 2017.

As you have been reading, have you identified an area of your soul, like the man with the lizard of lust, that needs to be transformed? Would you write that out and ask God for the courage to allow him to put that area to death by transformation?

Movements

Our souls are not static, but are always in motion, always responding to inputs that influence our thoughts, emotions, and choices. As we grow in understanding the movements of the soul, we can cooperate in the process of transformation. For example, there may be times when we feel confused and can't seem to think clearly or we are worrying and can't seem to stop fretting and dreading. Those are movements of the soul spiraling downward rather than upward in growth. Often that downward movement pulls us backward into the pain of the past and back into old patterns, beliefs, and attitudes.

The way we defeat downward spirals such as hopelessness and worry is by exchange. We set aside the old inclination and focus outside of ourselves, shifting our gazes onto the Lord and to good things outside of ourselves—a song, scripture, a friend, a book, a task, a walk in the park. This pivots our souls toward hope. We move up and out and forward, stepping toward the Lord, others, and the future. We turn to him, lifting our faces up, setting him before us (Ps 16:8). Expressed simply, the movement of our souls up and out facilitates healthy forward growth, but the movement of our souls down and inward impedes and stagnates growth.

An example of changing the downward spiral to upward movement is choosing to renew the mind (discussed in Chapter 3 as the ARC exercise). We arrest counterfeit thoughts and misbeliefs and renew our minds by exchanging lies for truth. Then as we continue to cultivate the renewed thoughts, truth and Christlike character is etched within us.

We can retrain our wills to engage the Lord, asking him to help us recognize patterns that start the downward spiral. As we learn to recognize the patterns and the catalysts that spark the downward movement, we can make other choices. The power of the cross and the resurrection are ours for this. We stop one habit by exchanging it for another. But it takes courage, patience, and effort. This exchange happens by grace and faith, knowing God is at work, whether we see it yet or not. In this way, new character qualities develop.

Philippe wrote in *The Way of Trust and Love* that we need to "discover and practice the inner attitudes, the dispositions of heart, which make us permeable to God's grace and attract it unfailingly. … God is faithful, and he loves us, and so we can find absolutely unfailing ways of attracting his grace."[136] God is our Father and when we lean into him with love and trust, he can't resist responding to us.

How do we develop the heart to sustain ourselves on the long road? By living in the reality of the Spirit of the living God, not focused on our own souls, but on the power of the Holy Spirit within. Otherwise, we strive and fail. We must live out of the reality of the indwelling Spirit who gives us the capacity to put to death our old habits and attitudes. In the dying is our rising!

We die in Christ to the old, the natural, and rise to the supernatural, the life of the Spirit within. Transformation is about the reality of the living Christ increasingly taking over more territory in our souls.

Practical Transformation

I'd like to illustrate practical transformation. In one recent season, my attention was drawn to the repetition of the goodness of the Lord in scriptures. David kept declaring his experience of knowing "the goodness of the Lord in the land of the living" (Ps 27:13 NIV). I knew God was pressing into me to receive that goodness, believing that surely goodness and mercy would follow me all my days (Ps 23:6). To have his goodness, I had to take in his goodness.

The goodness of God often refers to his abundant generosity and mercy as well as his excellence and uprightness of heart. His goodness is the very essence of his nature and is bound up in every way he expresses himself and everything he does. I began to want this beautiful character quality expressed within and through me. I wanted to be "full of goodness" but could see attitudes sorely lacking in goodness. Gradually I realized I could choose to respond in goodness and have his love poured into my heart

---

[136] Philippe, *The Way of Trust and Love* (N.P.: Scepter Publishers Inc., 2011), 36.

by the Holy Spirit (Rom 5:5). I began to set my heart in that direction, praying his goodness shown to me would be displayed more in me.

At the same time, I was keenly aware of some of my shortcomings, particularly in attitudes of impatience and judgment. But the more I immersed my thoughts, the meditation of my heart, on God's goodness toward me, the more I desired this same goodness to move out toward others through me. I began to seek after good for others (1 Thess 5:15; 2 Thess 1:11). As I yielded to the Holy Spirit, I noticed a change, that his goodness was trumping my impatience, my tendency toward frustration and criticism. My heart was more tender; I was seeing people through a new lens. His goodness, the fruit of the Holy Spirit, was growing inside me then moving out toward others. I was co-laboring with Christ to bring about new fruit so the virtues of goodness and forbearance began to increase within me. This is living the exchanged life: yielding up the old patterns of the soul for the life and presence of Christ. Exchanging old for new. This wasn't merely hopeful possibility; this was real transformation.

God is committed to transforming our lives, which means he's transforming our character.

- Where we have been reactive and defensive, we can become responsive, learning to ponder and listen, ruling our own hearts rather than reacting (Jas 1:19; Pr 16:32).
- Where we have been fretting and fearful, we can learn to take in his life and receive settled confidence and peace (Jn 14:1).
- Where we tend toward jealousy, we can begin to rejoice in good things for others (1 Cor 13:4-7).
- Where we have walked in judgmental pride, we learn to regard others well and forbear with them (Eph 4:2).
- Where we have been arrogant, we can choose humility (1 Pet 5:5).
- If gossip has had a prominent place in us, we can learn to rejoice with the truth (1 Cor 13:6).
- If we have been selfish, we can learn to practice a love that "does not seek its own" but the good of others (1 Cor 13:5 NASB1995).

- Where we tend toward pessimism and hopelessness, we can receive his infilling of hope (Rom 13:15).
- Where we have been flighty or avoidant we can learn to persevere and not give up in hard places (Jas 1:12).

To develop the new dispositions, we disengage the old tendencies by replacing them with new engagements. We engage the truth and the promises and the life within us. We are co-creators and collaborators with the operative power of his grace. In 2 Peter 1:5–8 (NIV), the apostle gives us an important key in this:

> For this very reason, *make every effort* to add to your faith goodness; and to goodness, knowledge; and to knowledge, self-control; and to self-control, perseverance; and to perseverance, godliness; and to godliness, mutual affection; and to mutual affection, love. For if you possess these qualities *in increasing measure*, they will keep you from being ineffective and unproductive in your knowledge of our Lord Jesus Christ. (Emphasis added.)

Peter indicates God is building character qualities in us, but we have to add our efforts to his grace for this or we will be lacking and shortsighted. It is not meant to be easy or automatic; it's meant to be a collaborative cultivation of our souls.

Character qualities have taken time to develop within and they will take time to re-form in us as we exchange the old for the new. What greatly helps and speeds the process is when we receive the light he is shining on the old attitudes of heart, allowing the Lord to convict our conscience so we can respond with repentance. We grant him access to heal old wounds and uproot old associated lies, biases, and limiting beliefs, and then with great deliberateness we take hold of living scripture, choosing to walk in the new way, developing new habits.

We have to be willing for him to expose and bring all things to the light. Often behind a certain dark inclination such as jealousy, anger, or hopelessness, are hidden lies. For instance: "I must protect myself from others or I'm not safe" may come up as cynicism, coldness, arrogance, or jealousy. As we ask the Holy Spirit what lies are still lurking, we can then renounce these and implant the truth, making the exchange. By the Spirit's help, we see where our hearts were trained in darkness and we bring them to the light for retraining.

Choices must be made. In doing so, we can either strive against things like lust or we can invite Jesus to be our strength and purity. We can receive him as our solid ground of goodness and righteousness and self-control. We aren't striving to be good, but instead receiving his goodness. This is not an experience, not an emotion, not just faith, but the living Christ, alive within us. It is a pattern of exchange of our natural life for his supernatural life.

In this exchange, we recognize Jesus lives in us and therefore all his character is available to us. We act on this recognition and we step forward with the steady faith that what we need is there. As we act, we will receive what we need to bring about change. And we do it with a firm intent to continue in faith, in patience, in perseverance. As we keep choosing, we begin to see real change.

Rather than waiting for emotions to be there before we act, we can acknowledge that Christ is in us and trust him to work new things in us, then step forward as an act of the will. The Lord meets us in our obedience as we choose to live in the new. Our character begins to be transformed so new grooves are etched in our souls, new patterns formed. We will begin to notice that the new things really are in us. As we take small steps along the way, they accumulate into larger transformation. We have to learn to take charge of our own attitudes—even a lifetime of them—toward life, self, and others. In doing so, we can learn new ways. His life is within us for this.[137]

Pause and Reflect

We live toward a virtue, receiving and developing it, while living against our natural bent until that character quality becomes a settled part of us, inherent in our character. To bring your natural bent into the light, make a list of the character qualities you would like the Lord to create or deepen within you (see Gal 5:22–23, 2 Pet 1:5–8). Where is he working just now?

---

[137] Waterman, lecture.

Prayer to Transform Dispositions

Lord, I confess to you these habits of temperament that I know don't reflect Jesus. I name _____ (fill in the blank). It is so easy for me to fall into this as my default. Reveal any hidden lies behind this character flaw, and any unknown painful memory that needs healing. I receive your forgiveness and healing.

I invite you to form the fruit of the Spirit in me as I exchange my old tendencies for your beautiful character. Lord, make me increasingly more like you, reflecting your glory and your nature. I thank you that there is already within me a whole place where you dwell.

Bring what you need to bring, Lord, to burn in me and create new and holy character. I ask grace for continued obedience and faithfulness, the empowering of your Spirit to keep stepping toward the new. I determine to put my effort into cooperating with you in this great adventure. In the name of Jesus.

Homework

Pick one of the nine character traits from the fruit of the Spirit listed in Gal 5:22–23: love, joy, peace, patience, kindness, goodness, faithfulness, gentleness, and self-mastery. Or choose a character quality such as gratefulness, generosity, hope, courage, justice, endurance, wisdom, or another such capacity.

For the next month, read about and meditate on that fruit of the Spirit or character quality, asking the Spirit to deepen that capacity within you.

Perhaps memorize one scripture verse related to that attribute. Make that verse your own so you can converse with the Lord in his language as you make progress against your natural bent.

Rejoice as you recognize transformation in your attitudes and outlook!

Recap

Our inner character qualities become deeply etched as we habitually choose to mature in Christ. Our maturity comes not by striving, but by receiving his goodness of character. By grace we can keep forming healthy patterns in our thinking, attitudes, emotions, and inclinations. We continue to exchange our ways of response, dying to the old, and opening the door for the Holy Spirit to establish his ways in us. By this process, we can learn to live in the reality of the indwelling Spirit who enables us increasingly to live demonstrating the character of Jesus. He has come to transform our whole souls.

12
CONCLUDING THOUGHTS

We have spent these chapters focusing on developing our souls, which is spiritual formation. Spiritual formation is the Spirit-led process of being changed and conformed to Christlikeness in the deepest places of our souls. There is no methodology in our path to wholeness; we are simply following the path of the one leading us in this formation. On the journey, we are engaged with Christ who lives within, forming and transforming us by his presence and his living words. We collaborate with him, directing our efforts to taking possession of our own land.

Spiritual formation is not just resisting sinful impulses but overcoming evil with good. We let go of the impostor and die to the old man who compensates for and covers sin and prevents access to God's love. We learn to practice Galatians 2:20, dying to the old self that we might be alive in him. We let go of idealized images of our own maturity and embrace the one who "gives the Spirit without measure" (Jn 3:34 NIV). We are opening our hearts, creating room, for the one who speaks and transforms and pours himself into us.

As we receive and continue to receive healing in our souls, we partner with God's formation of our souls through holy habits that keep fortifying the things that we have already received. There is no formula, but we help initiate conditions that reinforce and create an atmosphere that nurtures progress. Our holy habits provide a framework for spiritual formation. We are choosing by our efforts (which can only carry us so far) to exercise discipline. But, even more, we are opening ourselves to the supernatural power of the Holy Spirit, which is readily available to us.[138]

Abiding: Practicing the Presence

If there is a primary engine for spiritual formation, it is the habit of learning to abide in Christ. This means that by recognizing, understanding, and practicing the real presence of the Lord with us and within us we thrive. We are literally infused with his life, with his indwelling Spirit, enabling us to live on a supernatural plane in relationship with him.

R. A. Torrey wrote of the glory of having God's very life dwelling in us in a personal way.[139] When we comprehend this reality, when we truly believe God lives within us, we can receive from him this beautiful indwelling life. By receiving from him, we can then submit all the faculties of our souls, all that is within us, to God. We open our souls, every part of us, and learn more and more to recognize the Spirit's movements within us.[140] As we practice his presence, allowing him to possess us within, we yield to his rule and authority and others can see more of him in us. Kelly called this the "unworded but habitual orientation of all one's self about him who is the Focus."[141]

The more we recognize and practice his real presence, the more we avail ourselves of his riches and the more we come alive in his love. As this abiding in Christ becomes our principal pursuit, we begin to organize our whole life around practicing his presence.[142] Practicing his presence is about engaging with the Spirit, pursuing intimacy with him, and enjoying the life flowing between his heart and ours. Our transformation really hinges on this intimacy becoming increasingly ours. By faith, we can be conscious of his abiding presence with us.[143]

---

[138] John Mark Comer, *The Ruthless Elimination of Hurry*, 110.

[139] R. A. Torrey, *The Person and Work of the Holy Spirit* (1910; Project Gutenberg, 2009), 27, https://pdfroom.com/books/the-person-and-work-of-the-holy-spirit/9zk2ALeXgPJ.

[140] See *In the School of the Holy Spirit* by Jacques Philippe.

[141] Thomas R. Kelly, *A Testament of Devotion* (New York: Harper & Brothers, 1941), 44.

[142] Comer, 95.

[143] Andrew Murray, *The Secret of the Abiding Presence* (Fort Washington, PA: Christian Literature Crusade, rev. ed., 1998), 7.

Our prime responsibility is not to do something for God, it is to receive his love and learn to abide. If we don't abide in him, we'll constantly struggle to perform and therefore be subject to shame, doubt, and fear.

We have a position in Christ that is absolutely secure. There is already life in the vine, and the life supplied to the branch (us) is not based on what is going on around us or the feelings within us. It begins with the choice to engage our wills and acknowledge him. That choice becomes a habitual response which then becomes the movement of our souls looking to him and not to ourselves. We develop a habitual "knowing" of his presence, an intuitive sense. That, in brief, is the process of learning to practice his presence.

Abiding is about living closely, intimately connected with God, yet not necessarily *feeling* close to God. The whole idea is that there is Another who lives within me! This Christ lives within me and becomes the center of my being because he indwells me every moment. When we practice his presence we are simply calling this to mind.

Paul declared that the long-hidden mystery, now revealed in the gospel is this: "… Christ in you, the hope of glory" (Col 1:27 NASB). Our Christian spirituality is the experience of being empowered by a supernatural presence so that we are transformed from within. When our life is one of "… constant recognition of Another, the whole of life is transformed. It isn't a matter of continually allowing him to come into your life, because you have received him. But it is the recognition of another. … Another is the Person who inspires the prayers and imparts the faith and thinks the thoughts through our minds and expresses his compassion through our hearts. … Then you relax and say, 'This is what life is basically: Another living his life in me.'"[144] This is the antidote to living for self, dependent on self.

If God does all of this through us, are we merely puppets? Far from it. By his indwelling presence, he is making us our truest self, granting us divine power to be and to do. As we practice his presence, we are collaborating with him in establishing our identity and creating our destiny.

---

[144] Norman Grubb, *The Key to Everything* (Chicago: Moody Press, 1975), 34–35.

We have this confidence: "Christ is the final reality. Everything else has only a shadow existence. His love penetrates us and radiates through us."[145] So let us press on to know him, practicing his presence and becoming who we truly are in him, whole and healed.

Recap of the Book

By now I hope you have a richer perspective concerning both the anatomy of the soul and of spiritual formation within the soul. Our souls—all that is within us—are designed to operate in beautiful interdependence and harmony, each capacity and movement supporting the others. Transformation of the soul is a collaboration, a participation between our souls and the Spirit's wonderful enabling grace.

Although the different functions of the soul are not independent of one another, we have looked at the different faculties of the soul in distinct ways to aid in understanding the soul and its systems. As we understand the connections between how we act and think and feel and between the mutually supporting parts of our souls, we can more fully participate in our own development, learning to cultivate our wholeness.

The will, the organizing center of our personality, is essential to our vitality. As we exercise our wills to choose, we are able to develop our true voices. The will, operating as prime minister, orders and directs the other capacities while being influenced by them. Choosing to unite to God's will and ways is the highest use of our wills.

In our spiritual formation God begins to deal with our ways of knowing, and especially the deep patterns of our thought processes. We begin to realize the importance of our thought lives and recognize our vital responsibility to cultivate renewed minds in Christ. As we deal with strongholds in our thinking, with our wills we can learn to set our minds on thoughts of wholeness and holiness.

The *rational* mind directs our thoughts and beliefs and the *receptive* mind understands, receives, imagines, and activates our intuition. The receptive mind, both intuition and imagination, is about connection. It

---

[145] Walter Trobisch, *The Complete Works of Walter Trobisch* (Downers Grove, IL: InterVarsity Press, 1987), 644.

perceives and knows in a different way than the rational mind, but both are necessary for fully knowing and understanding. The receptive mind enters into and takes in what the rational mind can then put into words and execute. We need the reasoning rational mind, as well as the intuition and imagination of the receptive mind fully alive and open to the Holy Spirit.

The conscience acts as a guardian and protector of our souls, but can be malformed and become overly scrupulous or dulled. As the Lord brings understanding and healing to our conscience, we are renewed in our ability to walk in loving obedience and grace.

Appetites bridge the soul and the body. In our spiritual formation, we can make our bodies allies with our souls. When our appetites are in their place, a healthy intersect is created between the soul and the body and the energies of the body serve us rather than enslave us. Because our bodies are our domain, we take responsibility to govern them and honor them. We can refuse to idolize the importance of our appetites in our inner thought/ emotional lives and in our outer lives and relationships and choose instead to glorify God in our bodies.

Emotions bring color and responsiveness, a sense of aliveness. They are an essential and beautiful living energy of the soul and we need to understand how we are created so that we can express emotions well and in complement with the other parts of our souls. Emotions stir and move us, but they are not the true center we live from. We are to live by faith, and in the truth. By applying ourself to understand and take responsibility for our emotions, we can come alive with well-ordered emotions.

Desires motivate and propel our energies. Desire is a mighty force within our souls, a force that needs to be recognized, oriented, purified, surrendered, and strengthened. We can be fruitful in our desires and recover our true longings as we bring them into God's presence for their fulfillment in keeping with his ways.

To have a healthy sense of well-being is to have "personal vitality" and to be able to speak with a confident voice from our personhood. Our sense of being comes primarily from our early bond with mother when we experience nurture, validation, and security. Where we have been deprived of this early bond, we find healing as the living Spirit fills our inner being with his life. He enters our souls, healing earlier deprivations, bonding us to himself, and granting us a sense of fullness and being.

Our sense of being and the masculine-feminine present within each of us bring fullness of movement and being to our whole souls. The masculine and feminine qualities within the soul are essential, mysterious, and vital to our personal identity. As a revelation of God's true character, they reflect the integration of both initiation and response. They need to be understood, affirmed, balanced, and cultivated in their true expressions. Where we have lost God's design for the feminine and masculine within ourselves, he is more than able and willing to restore that to our souls.

Our deepest personality, our character, is formed as we come to wholeness in each of these capacities while choosing the way of the Lord. As we understand our secure position in Christ and learn to abide, continued healing and spiritual formation are possible. We are engaged with Christ who lives within, being formed and transformed by his presence. We collaborate, directing our efforts to constructing our souls. As we grow, choice by choice we form godly character as an essential faculty of our souls.

As we partner with the Lord, allowing him to deal with any darkness and brokenness within our souls, we rest in knowing he is the one who searches us, knows all that is within us, and is well able to bring us into healing and transformation. He becomes the center of our being, indwelling us in every part, radiating up through the whole self. It's his indwelling presence that makes the formation and transformation of our souls possible. Our part is to come into a shared participation in his life. He enters, transforms, and causes the voices of our souls to come fully alive. The Lord initiates and by grace and faith we respond in loving obedience. As Christ is formed in us, we become our true selves, masterpieces of his grace.

Prayer

Lord, seal this good work you have already accomplished in me and continue your healing of my soul. By your empowering grace, keep me on the path of holiness, developing the holy habits that enable you to work within me. Grant me a love for scripture. Help me to feed my mind and heart on it. Give me a devotion to surrender and worship, trusting you in all things. Enable me to practice your presence continually and learn to abide, to dwell constantly in the reality that I belong to you and have been made whole and holy in you. Thank you for your great love toward me, steadfast, faithful, and true all my days.

Hebrews 13:20 MSG

May God, who puts all things together,
> makes all things whole,

Who made a lasting mark through the sacrifice of Jesus,
> the sacrifice of blood that sealed the eternal covenant,

Who led Jesus, our Great Shepherd,
> up and alive from the dead,

Now put you together, provide you
> with everything you need to please him,

Make us into what gives him the most pleasure,
> by means of the sacrifice of Jesus, the Messiah.

All glory to Jesus forever and always!

Thank you for taking this journey with me to explore the voices of the soul. I am continually adding to the material through my website, blogs, podcasts, and YouTube videos. Although I no longer offer personal counseling, you can contact me for speaking engagements at my website: www.drbarbarabyers.com.

Acknowledgements

This book simply would not have been possible without the many authors and teachers I have drawn from. Primary among them are the works of Dr. Carla Waterman and Leanne Payne. In many chapters I have leaned on the lectures of Waterman, whose teachings first piqued my interest as she described the "anatomy of the soul." Many of the ideas and explanations here originated with her. And threaded throughout are also formative ideas from the writings and lectures of Payne, whose books I heartily recommend. I have also, with permission from publishers, borrowed from and built on the works of others, particularly Dr. Dallas Willard and C. S. Lewis.

My warmest thanks to my editor Deb Hvass who came in at the eleventh hour, probed with invaluable questions, and influenced the contours of the manuscript. Finally, I offer my deep gratitude to the small group of intercessors who committed to pray until the book was completed. Thank you my, friends!

Bibliography

Allender, Dan. *Leading with a Limp*. Colorado Springs, Co: WaterBrook Press, 2006.

Augustine of Hippo, St. *Confessions*, Volume II: Books 9–13, Loeb Classical Library 27. Translated by William Watts. Cambridge, MA: Harvard University Press, 1912.

Backlund, Wendy. *Victorious Emotions*. Redding, CA: Igniting Hope Ministries, 2017.

Banks, John Gaynor. *The Master and the Disciple*. St. Paul, MN: Macalester Park Publishing, 1954.

Bergner, Mario. *Setting Love in Order*. Grand Rapids, MI: Hamewith Books, an imprint of Baker Publishing Group, 1995.

Bessey, Sarah. *Jesus Feminist: An Invitation to Revisit the Bible's View of Women*. New York: Howard Books, 2013.

Billheimer, Paul. *Destined for the Cross*. Wheaton, IL: Tyndale House Publishers, 1982.

Brown, Brené. *Atlas of the Heart* (OverDrive ebook edition). New York: Random House, 2021.

Chambers, Oswald, *My Utmost for His Highest*. New York: Dodd, Mead & Company, 1935.

Chole, Alicia Britt. *Anonymous*. Nashville, TN: W Publishing Group, 2006.

Collier, Winn. *A Burning in My Bones*. Colorado Springs, CO: WaterBrook Press, 2021.

Colyn, Sarah. "Meditations on Wholeness in Christ" in Ministries of Pastoral Care newsletter (July 2017).

Comer, John Mark. *The Ruthless Elimination of Hurry.* Colorado Springs, CO: WaterBrook Press, a division of Penguin Random House LLC, 2019.

Crabb, Larry. *Fully Alive.* Grand Rapids, MI: Baker Books, 2013.

Elliot, Elisabeth. *The Mark of a Man.* Grand Rapids, MI: Revell, 1981.

Fénelon, Francois. *Let Go.* Amberson, PA: Scroll Publishing Co., 2007.

Grubb, Norman. *The Key to Everything.* Chicago: Moody Press, 1975.

Guardini, Romano. *The Lord.* Washington D.C.: Gateway Editions, 1954, 1982.

Harris, Nadine Burke. *The Deepest Well: Healing the Long-Term Effects of Childhood Adversity.* New York: Houghton Mifflin Harcourt, 2018.

Hession, Roy. *The Calvary Road.* Fort Washington, PA: Christian Literature Crusade, 1950.

Hooper, Walter, ed. *Collected Letters of C. S. Lewis, Vol. 1.* San Francisco: HarperSanFrancisco, 2004.

Kelly, Thomas R. *A Testament of Devotion.* New York: Harper & Brothers, 1941.

Kronman, Anthony T. *The Lost Lawyer: Failing Ideals of the Legal Profession.* Cambridge, MA: Harvard University Press, 1993.

Lake, Frank. *Clinical Theology.* London: Darton, Longman and Todd, 1966. This is now published by Emeth Press, Lexington, KY.

Lake, Frank. *Clinical Theology, Abridged* by Martin H. Yeomans. New York: Crossroad, 1987.

Lane, Belden C. "Jonathan Edwards on Beauty, Desire and the Sensory World" in *Theological Studies* 65 (2004): 44–72.

Lewin, Ann. "Entrance." In *Watching for the Kingfisher.* Norwich, UK: Hymns Ancient and Modern Ltd., 2009.

Lewis, C. S. *The Complete Chronicles of Narnia.* New York: HarperCollins Publishers, 2013.

Lewis, C. S. *The Great Divorce.* New York: Collier Books, 1946.

Lewis, C. S. *The Screwtape Letters.* New York: HarperOne, 1942, 1996.

Lewis, C. S. *The Weight of Glory.* New York: HarperOne, 1949, revised 1980.

MacNutt, Judith. Lecture at School of Healing Prayer Level III. Nov. 2–6, 2009.

Mason, Charlotte. *Ourselves* (eBook edition). Start Publishing LLC, (1905) 2012.

Menninger, Karl. *Whatever Became of Sin?* New York: Hawthorn Books, Inc., 1973.

Meyer, F. B. *The Secret of Guidance*, Hoboken, NJ: Start Publishing LLC, (1896) 2012. eBook edition.

Merriam-Webster Dictionary online. https://www.merriam-webster.com/dictionary/character.

Murray, Andrew. *The Secret of the Abiding Presence*. Fort Washington, PA: Christian Literature Crusade, rev. ed. 1998.

Naus, Eric. *God's Feminine Attributes*. July 5, 2011. https://www.moodychurch.org/gods-feminine-attributes/.

Outram, Ruth, Addiction, video 2021 at Bethel School of Supernatural Ministry, Redding, CA.

Packer, J. I. *Knowing God*. Downers Grove, IL: InterVarsity Press, 1993.

Payne, Leanne. *The Broken Image*. Grand Rapids, MI, Hamewith Books, an imprint of Baker Publishing Group, 1981, 1996.

Payne, Leanne. *Crisis in Masculinity*. Grand Rapids, MI: Hamewith Books, an imprint of Baker Publishing Group, 1985, 1995.

Payne, Leanne. *Listening Prayer*. Grand Rapids, MI: Hamewith, a division of Baker Publishing Group, 1994.

Payne, Leanne. *The Healing Presence*. Grand Rapids, MI: Hamewith Books, an imprint of Baker Publishing Group, 1989, 1995.

Payne, Leanne. *Restoring the Christian Soul Through Listening Prayer*. Wheaton, IL: Crossway Books, a division of Good News Publishers, 1991.

Payne, Leanne. Lecture on Listening Prayer at School of Pastoral Care Ministries. Wheaton, IL, July 1996.

Pertuit, Mark. Lecture series at the School of Pastoral Care Ministries, Wheaton, IL, July 27, 2010.

Philippe, Jacques. *In The School of the Holy Spirit*. Strongsville, OH: Scepter Publishers Inc., 2007.

Philippe, Jacques. *Interior Freedom*. Strongsville, OH: Scepter Publishers Inc., 2007.

Philippe, Jacques. *Searching for and Maintaining Peace*. Staten Island, New York: ST PAULS, 2002.

Philippe, Jacques. *The Way of Trust and Love*. Strongsville, OH: Scepter Publishers Inc., 2011.

Ratushinskaya, Irina. *Grey is the Color of Hope*. (A. Kojevnikov, trans.). New York: Alfred A. Knopf, Inc., 1988.

Ratushinskaya, Irina. *In the Beginning*. New York: Alfred A. Knopf: 1991.

Rolheiser, Ronald. *The Holy Longing: The Search for a Christian Spirituality*. New York, NY: Image Books, an imprint of the Crown Publishing Group, a division of Penguin Random House, Inc., 1998, 1999, 2014.

Ryan, Barbara Shlemon. *Healing the Hidden Self*. Notre Dame, IN: Ave Maria Press, 1982/2005.

St. Mark's Coptic Orthodox Church. "The Characteristics of Alexandrian Theology." NJ: Jersey City, website of St. Mark's Coptic Orthodox Church. Accessed September 9, 2022. (https://www.copticchurch.net/patrology/schoolofalex/I-Intro/chapter2.html).

Scazzero, Peter. *Emotionally Healthy Spirituality*. Grand Rapids, MI: Zondervan, 2006, 2017.

Spurgeon, Charles H. *The Spurgeon Archive* (https://archive.spurgeon.org/treasury/ps139.php).

ten Boom, Corrie. *The Hiding Place*. Washington Depot, CT: Chosen Books, 1971.

ten Boom, Corrie. *Tramp for the Lord*. Ada, MI: Revell Co., 1974.

Therapon Institute. *Spirit, soul and body: A total approach to recovery for hurting and healing people*. Crockett, TX: Therapon Institute, Inc., n.d.

Torrey, R. A. *The Person and Work of the Holy* Spirit. Digital reprint of 1910 Fleming H. Revell Company edition, Project Gutenberg, 2009. https://pdfroom.com/books/the-person-and-work-of-the-holy-spirit/9zk2ALeXgPJ.

Tozer, A. W. *The Mystery of the Holy Spirit*. Newberry, FL: Bridge-Logos, 2007.

Tozer, A. W. *Tozer on the Almighty God: A 365-day Devotional,* January 8 reading. Chicago: Moody Bible Institute, 2004, 2020.

Trobisch, Walter. *The Complete Works of Walter Trobisch*. Downers Grove, IL: InterVarsity Press, 1987.

Vallotton, Kris. Sermon at Bethel Church, Redding, CA, August 2, 2021.

Waterman, Carla. *Capacities and Motions of the Soul*, lecture series recorded at Church of the Resurrection, Wheaton, IL, 1999.

Waterman, Carla A. *Songs of Assent*. Wheaton, IL: WaterManuscripts LLP, 2009.

West, Christopher. *At the Heart of the Gospel*. New York, NY: Image Books, an imprint of the Crown Publishing Group, a division of Random House, Inc., 2012.

West, Christopher. *Theology of the Body Explained*. Boston, MA: Pauline Books & Media, 2003.

Whyte, Alexander. *Lord Teach Us to Pray*. Yuma, CO: Jawbone Digital, 2012 (first published in 1922). jawbonedigital.com.

Willard, Dallas. *Renovation of the Heart*. Colorado Springs, CO: NavPress, 2002.

Printed in the United States
by Baker & Taylor Publisher Services